The Learning Dimension

About the Author

Margaret Dale is a human resource consultant. She is the author of *Developing Management Skills* (Kogan Page, 1999), *The People Dimension* (Blackhall Publishing, 1999) and co-author of *The Business Dimension* (Blackhall Publishing, 1999)

The Learning Dimension

MARGARET DALE

BLACKHALL
Publishing

This book was typeset by
Gough Typesetting Services for

Blackhall Publishing,
27 Carysfort Avenue,
Blackrock, Co. Dublin,
Ireland.

and

Blackhall Publishing,
2025 Hyperion Avenue,
Los Angeles,
CA 90027,
USA.

Email: blackhall@eircom.net
Website: www.blackhallpublishing.com

© Margaret Dale, 2002

A catalogue record for this book is available from the British Library

ISBN: 1 842180 26 6

Printed in Ireland by
ColourBooks Ltd

To Tom, who encouraged me to start writing; to Alex, who trusted me and modelled how learning can achieve considerable change and benefits for others; and to the many active Learners, whose humility and attainments provided the examples for this book and act as Role Models for us all.

Contents

Introduction

Learning is often taken to mean education or training. It is used as a synonym for teaching or lecturing and sometimes it is difficult to see why it is being used, when one of these words would do instead. When it is used in its proper sense, the difference is stark. Learning is about the achievements of an individual and the processes used to attain them. Teaching, lecturing and training and what other people do to help (or in some cases hinder) learning of others.

In this book, the focus is on the individual. It is intended to provide an explanation of how learning takes place and what can improve it so that you, the reader, can develop your learning abilities and perhaps, in gaining greater insight, provide more effective support to others.

It is therefore intended to be practical and the ideas proposed are based on what has been seen to work. However, as learning is individual and can be influenced by the context in which it takes place, these ideas should only be seen as suggestions. It is likely that you will need to find out, by having a go, what will work best for you.

Acknowledgements

I would like to thank Beatrice, for reading and amending my manuscript (in doing so she learnt how to format endnotes), Roger, for his endless patience and understanding, Bruce, for being a faithful companion, and Mother, for:

Good, better, best
Never let it rest
'Til your good is better
And your better best

She repeatedly tells me "so long as you have done your best, no one can expect anything more": a wonderful message to guide our progress on our learning journey.

Chapter 1

What is Learning?

INTRODUCTION

What is learning? A simple enough question you might think. But the answer is far from easy to give. Providing a satisfactory reply depends as much on who is doing the asking and what sort of answer is expected, as on the degree of knowledge and understanding of the responder. An educationalist will expect one kind of definition, a psychologist another. A learning technologist – a new breed of academic – will expect to be given yet another type of reply. While the learner – the person at the centre of the process and recipient of the experience – will want a totally different type of answer.

This book is not designed for learning professionals. It is aimed at people who want to make the most of their own learning and help that of others. You, the reader may have some theoretical knowledge and want to add to it. Or you might be just beginning your exploration of the subject and see this as a starting point. So this book provides some background and aims to guide you towards gaining additional insight into what helps or hinders your learning. Most importantly, its primary purpose is to provide practical help and ideas on how to make learning easier, more enjoyable and more successful for you and those you help.

This will be done by focusing on the reality of learning. Theory will only be used to supply explanation and aid understanding. But we will not necessarily adhere blindly to theoretical models for there is no right or wrong way to learn. The best learning methods are those most appropriate for achieving the desired outcome, as defined by the person doing the learning. All too often, what is regarded as the best way of learning is specified by the people providing it or even worse by the people telling those supplying it what to do. We will not be prescriptive here. Rather we will consider the practicalities and discuss the circumstances that foster effective learning and the barriers that get in the way.

Chapter 1 will begin by exploring the concept of learning and how it is interpreted. There is no wish to be pedantic but at this opening stage it is a risk worth running, for without initial clarity there is a danger that we will later flounder in a swamp of jargon and become confused by words that seem interchangeable but that in fact have different meanings. To avoid this we will start by looking at some of the formal definitions.

Chapter 2 will consider how different people learn and the conditions that best support personal style and individual preferences. We will also discuss the importance of gaining feedback in the learning process. Feedback is information essential for monitoring your progress. It highlights where achievements are being made and where further practise is required. Without it, it is very difficult to gauge how well you are doing and even if you are heading in the right direction. However, giving good quality feedback is not easy and accepting it can be equally difficult.

Chapter 3 moves on to look at the barriers to learning. Some of these exist in the environment in which the learning is taking place as well as where it is to be applied. Some obstacles are constructed by the people around us, sometimes deliberately but most often unwittingly. In the case of the latter, simple negotiations can be enough to remove the barrier. In the case of the former, a different approach may be merited. Often, however, the biggest barriers to learning are put in place by ourselves. We stop our own progress for a host of reasons. Understanding what these are and why we do it to ourselves is the first step in removing them.

Removing them alone will not necessarily be easy or improve the quality of the learning; further action may be required. We will look at some of the practical steps that you might take to make your learning and that of others easier. That does not mean it will not be hard work. Sometimes learning requires effort and may even involve some pain. But there is no need to climb a mountain if climbing a hill will result in the same quality of outcome. Advances in technology and the Lifelong Learning campaign have led to a massive increase in learning aids and resources and a better understanding of the process, especially the learning of adults. However, there is some danger of medium taking over from the message. But if a particular medium stimulates learning and provides some enjoyment in its own right, there is no harm in using it. We will consider how best to exploit some of the newer resources to ensure that the desired learning is achieved.

Chapter 4 is devoted to the consideration of the factors that help individuals learn effectively. The wish to promote Lifelong Learning is in danger of focusing on delivery and resources without considering the skills of an effective learner and the sorts of conditions they need to support their efforts. It is important that the motives for learning are taken into account, especially those of adults returning to learning. We also need to be aware of the nature of the risks involved, the support required and the chance to practise new skills.

Finally, chapter 5 examines a range of techniques that may be useful for you to try, if you are not already familiar with them from your previous experiences. Most of them do not involve formal education or training activities. The emphasis is on the practical steps you can take without recourse to external or extra resources, so we will discuss how you can incorporate learning into your approaches to everyday work or draw on facilities readily available. We will also look at how you can work with other people whose desired outcome is similar to your own. The content may be different but the end product – an increase in knowledge and/or skill – will be shared.

You will be offered suggestions about how your own learning may be improved and how you can help other people learn better. The examples given are all brief summaries of the experiences of real people. However, in the end it is really up to you to decide what to do, if anything at all. We are all responsible for our own learning and have the ability to decide what to do about it. Resources, support and assistance of others help enormously but they are not essential. We all have the ability to decide whether to engage in learning and whether to help other people or not. Learning how to learn better is within our grasp and is our choice whether we do so or stay the same. Hopefully this book will help you become a more able learner whose enjoyment of the process is increased.

LEARNING DEFINED

Learning: the word applied to both the content and the process of moving from a state of unknowing and incompetence to one of awareness, understanding and competence. The stages involved can be represented simply in the following diagram:

Figure 1.1: Stages of Learning

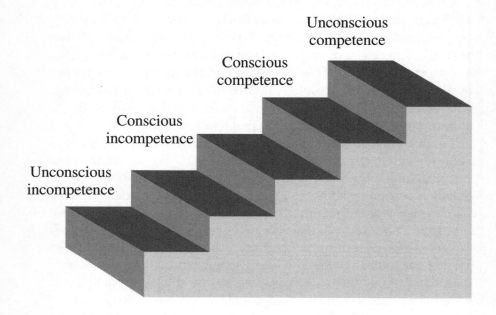

The end result – the state of unconscious competence – will have been achieved from:

- a change in the existing level of knowing and ability to do
- an increased insight into self, other people and situations
- the application of outcomes and practice during the early stages
- the process by which knowledge will have been created though the transformation of experience.

Learning is a vital human process, essential for survival and fundamental to evolution. Learning is about acquiring and extending knowledge, developing and improving skills, and forming and questioning attitudes. It is possible for learning to take place in any setting, under any set of circumstances, in the company of others or alone. Learning does not need to be formal or organised but it does need to be aimed at achieving some outcome, for *growth without a purpose is the ideology of the cancer cell*.

Learning can be the result of serendipity – happy accidents – and can also be the unintended consequence of other actions. It can be unplanned but to claim that it has happened it needs to be put into practice or used in some way. We will discuss the implications of this in our exploration of what learning is in practice. While theory can be used to give insight for this, essentially this book aims to help you understand what learning means to you and what you can do to get better in your own learning and helping others with theirs.

A PROCESS AND AN OUTCOME

Learning has two facets. Mostly the word is used to describe the result of an activity or an event – the outcome. For example the question "what did you learn today" is often posed to children returning from school or to an employee calling in to their workplace on their way home after attending a course. It can also be asked at the end of any normal day. Each opportunity provides the chance to do something in a different way or gain new insight. Yet more often than not, these opportunities pass by without their potential for providing learning being recognised. Change and the challenge of different experiences are frequently unwelcome interruptions to the stability of our world – they disturb the status quo. A different attitude can transform these from threats into chances for developing skills and adding to the individual's bank of experiences.

An important way of making the most use of the opportunities to gain insight and develop skills is to reflect hard upon them and with purpose. You can access this type of deep thinking by asking questions of yourself and persuading others to discuss daily occurrences. For example after completing a piece of work, ask yourself or a colleague what was learnt from the experience:

- Why was the task completed in that particular way?
- If it had been done in any other way, would a different – better or worse – result have been achieved?
- Would the work have been harder or easier? Would it have taken a longer or shorter period of time to complete?
- If someone else had done it, what would have happened?
- Would it have been done at all?

Learning can also describe the process used to achieve the outcome. Sometimes we risk confusion by not distinguishing between the process and the outcome. *The Oxford Concise English Dictionary* states that "learning" is: *knowledge acquired by study.* Yet "learn" is also to:

> . . . gain knowledge of or skill in by study, experience or being taught; acquire or develop a particular ability (learn to swim); commit to memory (will try to learn your names); be informed about; become aware of by information or from observation; receive instruction, acquire knowledge or skill.

It is clear from the various concepts used to define the terms that the outcome – knowledge or skill – is mixed up with the different ways of acquiring – study, experience and being taught.

Learning as a process is affected by many factors that can enhance or detract from the achievement of the desired outcome. These factors can be the learner or part of the environment in which the learning is taking place. They can be generated by other people, both co-learners and the people facilitating the process. The term "facilitator" is increasingly being used to replace the word "teacher", "tutor" or "trainer". A facilitator theoretically should be someone who makes the learning process easy. This suggests that they understand the process as well as having some competence in the content. We can all remember teachers who were brilliant in their subject but hopeless in helping others learn. We may also have come across others who were not so well informed but very able to help learners acquire the required knowledge or gain the skills. This is proven by the fact that the very best opera singers go regularly to singing coaches.

Sometimes the behaviour and attitude of trainers, tutors and teachers can get in the way or even stop learning from happening at all. Sometimes, on the other hand, a learning outcome can be achieved from a dysfunctioning process. Learning does not always have to be easy or even enjoyable for a result to be achieved. Athletes have a phrase – *there is no gain without pain* – that can apply equally well to learning. Learning can be hard work – it requires effort. Particularly in self-development, gaining insight and changing behaviour can come about from accepting that previous levels of performance may have been ineffective, antisocial or below the expected level. Despite the pain, however, the results can be worth the exertion.

Recognising the difference between learning processes and learning outcomes is important, as they require separate consideration. Disentangling them means that attention can be given to:

- what is to be achieved – the objectives will determine the content of the learning. Level and quantity of the content should take account of the individuals, their needs, previous experiences of learning and their levels of attainment

- how the learning is to be achieved – the processes chosen should also take account of the individuals involved, their previous experience and preferred modes of learning. The circumstances and resources available to support the learning will also be factors.

We will discuss the practical implications of all these at greater length in the following pages. Getting them right makes the difference between good learning that results in tangible and valuable outcomes but muddling them up can mean that neither is addressed properly and opportunities for maximising the outcomes are reduced. Getting them wrong risks turning people off learning all together.

LEARNING IS NOT ATTENDING COURSES

Learning does not always take place in the classroom or training centre. In fact some, such as Illich, have argued that *education is the death of learning*.[1] The formality and rigidity of the process can stand in the way of achieving the desired outcome and limit the learner. Because the content is controlled by the provider, it may not be relevant or even of interest to the learner. For sure, some people learn very well in formal or theoretical settings. They are able to take ideas, conceptualise them, store them and later translate them into action. Others prefer to watch someone demonstrate what the idea means in practice and then draw on theory to explain the whys and where-fors. Both are equally valid and may well result in the same outcome. They are simply two ways of achieving the same ends.

---

[1] Illich, I, *Deschooling Society* (Harmondsworth: HarperCollins) 1971.

Often, it seems that it is assumed that everyone learns in exactly the same way. Certainly the education of young people has in recent years been governed by ideological as well as professional considerations. In the heat of the debate the cognitive processes of individuals seem to receive little attention. Emphasis is being given to passing tests and examinations and to league tables. Enthusing young people about learning and equipping them with the skills needed to continue to learn throughout life are forced into second place. The needs of the learner deserve more attention. This is particularly so for adults returning to learning whose previous experience of education may have been less than positive. Although teaching styles have moved from *teacher-centred,* whole class instruction to *student-centred*, self-determined and group work, there are always casualties – individuals whose own learning style does not fit into that of the majority or the approach in use at the time. There is a danger that they are regarded as being mavericks or simply educational failures. Their faith in their own abilities to learn can be destroyed and they may become "closed down" as learners. Unless of course something is done to keep them "switched on".

Fortunately, Adult Education often takes account of past experiences and is well able to re-engage the disaffected. However, there is considerable pressure towards economy of scale. This forces the use of methods known to work adequately well most of the time for most people. But one size does not fit all. Learning, fundamentally and essentially, is personal and what works well for one person may not work at all for another. We will discuss further how the mismatch between personal learning style and learning method can prevent the achievement of the common goal – learning.

LEARNING IS NOT BEING TAUGHT

The definitions given above suggest that the word *learning* can be used as a synonym for *teaching*. This may be due to much of the research and theorising coming mainly from the perspective of the provider rather than that of the recipient. *Learning* is presented as a process to which an individual is subjected (willingly or otherwise) and the key player (the actor) is the teacher or provider. The subject (the learner) is a passive party. Even when learner-centredness is claimed, the subject's viewpoint does not seem to be fully considered in most of the textbooks.

The efficiency and effectiveness (and economy of time, effort and cost) of the delivery is measured from the point of view of the teacher. The choice of content is dictated by the wishes of those setting the learning agenda (often nationally laid down syllabi) as opposed to the interests and needs of the learner. The value of the learning from the subject's point of view, their reasons for engaging and desired outcomes do not appear to figure largely. Even though the reasons for this approach can be understood in schools, justifying a standardised approach is a little more difficult when applied to experienced adults.

This view can be found in the *Declaration on Learning*.[2] This was written by a group of highly experienced thinkers and supporters of others' learning and states that:

> Our understanding of learning has generally been restricted to formal teaching and training. Learning is often seen as unrelated to daily life and work. Systems of accreditation are sometimes used as a way of unfairly discriminating between individuals and are often felt to be irrelevant to real needs.

QUALIFICATIONS ARE NOT PROOF OF LEARNING

There is no denying the value of qualifications. In the world of work they are a currency, signifying achievement and ability. They are so valuable that some people claim to have achieved qualifications they have not. Job application forms frequently have a space for the applicants to list their examination passes and certificates so that employers can make assumptions about their level of competency and their potential standard of performance. During employment, their acquisition can result in pay increases, the assignment of more interesting work or promotion. Alternatively, not having any

---

[2] The Learning Declaration Group is an informal group of leading authors, researchers and practitioners including John Burgoyne, Ian Cunningham, Bob Garratt, Peter Honey, Andrew Mayo, Alan Mumford, Michael Pearn and Mike Pedler.

qualifications can be taken as an indictor of deficiency, lack of ability or intelligence, or some form of failure.

Qualifications are now regarded as being so important that the Government, CBI and TUC joined to establish the National Education and Training Targets (now National Learning Targets). The intent is to use these to raise the general level of qualifications in the population as a whole. The targets include provision for increasing the number of young people participating in higher education and widen the participation of those not traditionally found in higher education. At the sub-degree level, the targets cover both academic and vocational qualifications.

The National Vocational Qualifications (NVQs) were originally introduced in Britain to create a framework which would encompass the myriad of non-academic qualifications. Previously, these had been awarded by many different bodies, each using their own terms and standards. There was widespread confusion as it was not clear how each qualification related to the others in similar and different occupations. The idea behind the NVQs was not to do away with the separate awarding bodies but to provide a coherent structure across them all for each major occupation. The structure now comprises of five levels: Level I is very basic, almost entry level; Level II represents basic skills; Level III is for more experienced or complex areas of work; Level IV is professional; and Level V is for work in a senior role requiring considerable experience and competence. Thus it is possible now to say that someone with Level II in Hairdressing is broadly as competent as a Level II Motor Mechanic.

From their name, it is obvious that NVQs are intended to be acquired at work. This need not always be the case and, especially at Level II, they can be achieved in the classroom or training centre. Regardless of where the learning is acquired, the candidates' level of competence is assessed through the production of task-related evidence. Normally the evidence is collected in a portfolio which is assessed by a trained assessor. There are no examinations. Some awarding bodies have combined the use of portfolios with more traditional forms of assessment, such as assignments, case studies and tests of knowledge to monitor progress and the acquisition of underpinning knowledge as well as skills.

The decision to use portfolios as the main vehicle for assessment was intended to take account of those whose previous experience of education was less positive. It was acknowledged that the thought of taking examinations might prevent these people from entering the assessment process, even when their performance at work may be considerably higher than that required for the NVQ. There has been some considerable success over the years in encouraging people who, for whatever reason, left school with no qualifications to work towards obtaining NVQs. As well as attaining the tradable, valuable commodity of a qualification, they have found that their self-confidence and self-esteem have also grown.

Most of the efforts made in Britain to encourage people back to learning take the form of structured initiatives. For example career development loans and individual learning accounts are to help people pay the fees they would not otherwise be able to afford. The Employee Development Schemes run by some employers encourage staff to take part in courses, most often those leading to the achievement of some identifiable learning objective such as a qualification. Many of the programmes designed to help people back to employment are run in training centres and are designed to lead to the acquisition of NVQs as well as a job. The Campaign for Lifelong Learning was launched in the late 1990's with support from all main stakeholders to persuade, cajole and support adults back to learning. When the Labour Party campaigned in 1997 on the platform of "Education, education, education", the politicians were not just talking about children and schools.

Effort is increasingly being made to provide resources to aid and support learning in its many different forms. Some companies are setting up Learning Resource Centres for their employees to augment formal training. The resources may include computers as well as other material such as videos, tapes, books and multi-media learning packs. Public libraries and other places, including sports centres and pubs, are being extended to develop such resource centres. The Internet provides access to material and information from which people can learn by purposefully seeking the answer to a question or by stumbling on something that is interesting. On-line learning packages are now available, many provided through Learning Direct. We are in the information technology era and those not engaged in some form of learning are out of step.

The UK government surveys a huge range of everyday activities and produces statistics to chart changes and monitor the effects of policies. One of its publications is the National Adult Learning Survey. Each year this records the level of participation in "Learning" and monitors progress towards the achievement of the National Learning Targets. In 1998, it was decided to include other forms of learning in addition to course-based activity.

Sadly, those not participating in any type of learning are called "non-learners". This denies the existence of learning other than that falling within the scope of the definition and does not give credit to the learning that goes on informally. Many of the references found in the text books describe informal learning as the additional learning activities undertaken by those involved in formal processes or organised activity (for example mentor schemes, community volunteer programmes, out of school activities); few describe the processes that occur during learning.

Learning takes place in many ways, at other times in addition to formal activities. Using the definitions given at the beginning of this chapter, it can be seen that any event that leads to a change in behaviour, level of skill or mode of thinking can be described as learning. A chance remark overheard on the bus can be sufficient to introduce a new idea and lead to a period of reflection that results in a change of attitude and different behaviour. We all have the capacity to learn if we want. Even those very resistant to taking part in any form of formal learning are prepared to accept that they can learn in the University of Life. Most people engage in some form of learning throughout their lives. Only those totally closed to new ideas or any form of change in their behaviour can really be called non-learners.

One of the challenges in encouraging adults back to learning is to give recognition to the full range of learning activities that people engage in. Whether it is necessary to find ways of codifying and qualifying them is another matter. Possibly formal qualification is not necessary but acceptance that learning takes place in situations other than formal settings is crucial. Another challenge is finding ways to bring back those previously failed by the education and formal learning structures. To do this we need to understand why and how adults learn.

WHY DO ADULTS START TO LEARN?

Perhaps the more important question is, *What stops people learning?* It is generally believed that very young children are naturally curious and eager to learn. Kelly, an American psychologist writing in the 1950's, maintained that all people are *"natural scientists"*, striving to understand and predict events.[3] We do not like uncertainty, preferring to consider the likely course of events and prepare ourselves. We ask questions of others with more experience, find out, prepare ourselves and practise beforehand so we are not caught unawares. We prefer to expend the effort required in rehearsal than experience the stress incurred by being unready.

If this is true, why do people lose the ability and inclination to learn? As noted above, writers such as Illich[4] and Freire[5] believe that, as education is a process of social control, people become institutionalised in their learning habits. Many become alienated by the processes used or they are taught to limit their learning abilities. But not all adults lose their inclination for learning and it is possible to re-engage those who have stopped learning. Something is working well for the many people who have benefited from the introduction of NVQs, employee development schemes and the increased availability of learning resources. Is it possible to learn from these achievements and work out what might help those still not engaged in learning?

Tough[6] identifies thirteen reasons for learning which can be grouped into three main categories:

1. the importance of having a goal and the need for knowledge or skills to achieve it

2. a source of puzzlement or curiosity and the need to acquire knowledge to solve the question

3. having a desire to learn.

---

[3] Kelly, G A, *A Theory of Personality: The Psychology of Personal Constructs* (New York: Norton) 1955.

[4] Illich, I, *Deschooling Society* (Harmondsworth: Penguin) 1971.

[5] Freire, P, *Pedagogy of the Oppressed* (New York: Continuum) 1970.

[6] Tough, A M, *The Adult Learning Projects* (Ontario Institute for Studies in Education Research in Education) Series No 1, 1971.

Other writers suggest that individuals develop a sense of some form of dissatisfaction with the status quo and/or they experience the desire to alter some aspects of their lives. This "pain" provides the motivation to engage in action to make changes and learning can occur as a result. Evidently, the individual does not have to depend on a classroom or other formal learning situation.

HOW DOES LEARNING HAPPEN?

To answer this question we need to draw on theory. There are several schools of thought that have considered this question. The main ones include education theory, psychology and sociology but others, such as behavioural science and even political science, have contributions to make to the debate. There has also been a lot of research carried out by those involved in providing and understanding learning at work, particularly as it can be applied to managers.

The main foci of the theories relevant to learning at work are summarised in Figure 1.2. If you are interested in finding out more about these you may wish to refer to some of each subject's introductory text books.

Understanding the different standpoints may be interesting and in themselves they offer insight into the processes of learning, but they do not necessarily provide practical guidance on ways of re-engaging the disaffected or encouraging the reluctant learner. Neither do they provide simple ways of helping you improve your own learning nor guide you when supporting the learning of others.

You cannot learn for someone else. Learning is essentially a process internal to the individual. However, there is a lot that can be done to create an environment that is conducive to learning and supportive of the process. We need to remember, however, that actions of others can create barriers and actively serve to dissuade people from learning. For example a manager who constantly finds fault with every piece of work and decries staff's efforts will hardly create a climate in which people are prepared to take the risks involved in learning new skills. However, a manager who is prepared to let staff try out ideas, let them practise and refine their skills, who accept that mistakes happen and is able to provide constructive feedback is more likely to have teams able to learn new ways of working and adapt their methods.

Figure 1.2: Relevant Theories

Psychology:
- development of mental/cognitive skills
- development of personality
- motivation and needs of individual
- learnt behaviour

Sociology:
- concept of role and self
- self-identity and self-efficacy
- relationships with others
- impact on others
- group dynamics and power bases
- conditioned and learnt behaviour

Education:
- influenced by child development theories
- needs to recognise experience of adults to help them return to formal learning
- main focus on issues of delivery
- learning aimed at achievement of pre-specified aims and objectives
- transfer to work secondary

Development:
- influenced by psychology and sociology
- emphasis on managers professionals to a lesser extent
- includes personal development to a lesser extent than work related behaviour
- worker development and empowerment more concerned with needs of job (even learning to learn) than personal growth

Training:
- similar to education
- influenced by military methods
- centres on vocational skills, short-term and organisational needs
- behaviour modification and socialisation mainly aimed at meeting the needs of the job
- interfaces with development

These practical tips are known to facilitate learning. While they may guide your action and approach to managing your staff, they do not necessarily explain how learning happens. Kolb carried out research into the process and his findings have been used as the basis for much of the thinking underpinning the design of learning programmes aimed at adults.[7] His terminology has been adapted for British consumption by Peter Honey and Alan Mumford.[8] Kolb's cycle comprises four stages, each of which needs to be completed. They build each on each and reinforce learning. They also represent differences in preferred learning styles.

Figure 1.3: Kolb's Learning Cycle

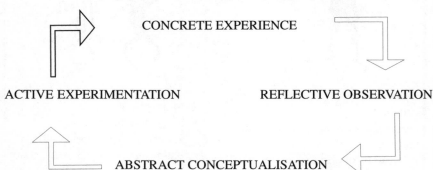

CONCRETE EXPERIENCE

ACTIVE EXPERIMENTATION   REFLECTIVE OBSERVATION

ABSTRACT CONCEPTUALISATION

Concrete experience, as it implies, means that the learner does something: they have a go at doing the job; they try a new skill; they read about a new idea.

Reflective observation means that the learner stands back from the experience: they think about what has happened; they might talk about it to another person.

Abstract conceptualisation means gaining insights into what has happened and drawing conclusions that might be applied to other similar situations.

---

[7] Kolb, D A, *Experiential Learning: Experience as the Source of Learning and Development* (Hemel Hempstead: Prentice-Hall) 1985.

[8] Honey, P & A Mumford, *The Manual of Learning Styles* (Maidenhead: Peter Honey) 1982.

Active experimentation is the stage when those ideas are put into practice, new skills tried out and new behaviours trialled. On the basis of this subsequent experience the cycle begins again.

This simple model provides very practical guidance on how to use everyday events as vehicles for learning. It also stresses that experience alone is not sufficient for learning to happen. The subsequent stages are essential for the meaning of the experience to be understood, its more general application considered and new thinking or behaviour reinforced through practice. Practice, the opportunities for being slow, making mistakes and receiving feedback tend to be neglected in the high-speed world in which we now live. Even though technology has speeded up the delivery of learning resources and even though communications may have become faster, sadly the human brain is still driven by the speed of evolution. Learning takes time.

Kolb's Learning Cycle guides the actions of those supporting the learning of others as it underpins the roles of a job instructor, a coach and a mentor. These can all create opportunities for experience and aid the reflective stages by allowing critical questioning, encouraging deeper thinking and suggesting alternatives. The four stages also indicate preferred ways of learning. These may influence the behaviour of the learning supporter; they certainly influence the behaviour of the learner.

1. An *activist* learns best by doing. They do not have the patience to read instructions or manuals. They want to get their hands dirty, get stuck in.

2. A *reflector* on the other hand prefers to take their time. They like to be able to think about things and mull them over before tentatively trying new ways.

3. A *theorist* is better dealing with ideas and concepts. They discuss and consider alternatives. They seek additional information and weigh pros and cons. They conduct trials and pilots before trying things out for real.

4. A *pragmatist* meanwhile focuses on the practicalities. They think about the problems and benefits and are very good at identifying potential pitfalls or weaknesses in the ideas.

Once you understand how you learn best, it is easier to appreciate other people's learning styles. This insight will help you structure learning opportunities to best suit individual preferences. This means playing to your strengths but it does not mean you should ignore those styles you prefer less. It does indicate where you need to improve but suggests the type of learning activity that will make it easier for you to learn. For example there is little point in a predominant activist trying to improve their reflector learning style by sitting in a darkened room pondering on deep thoughts. They would be better suited to a structured, interactive exercise that, step by step, took them further into active thinking.

We will discuss learning styles in greater length later and provide more detailed examples of how they may be used to build on strengths and use weaker areas. The aim is to develop a learner with a broad range of learning skills. These will equip you with the ability to make the most of every opportunity presented to you and become flexible in your learning. As an all-round learner you will be able to choose what to do and how to react to new situations. Having choice and options puts you in a powerful position and enables you to determine your own future.

For the time being that is sufficient theory about learning. As you may have already appreciated, learning is not just a cerebral activity. To be an active learner you need to do things. And as a supporter of others' learning, being passive is insufficient; you need to do things to help them.

SUMMARY

Learning is hard work; it takes effort and determination. You need to apply yourself to the task in hand and concentrate. Learning can be challenging and at times painful, especially if you have to confront situations you find difficult and uncomfortable. It may be stressful and demanding. It can absorb you and become compelling. Learning can take over your way of life and you can easily become addicted.

Learning is fun, it is enjoyable and it can lead to unimagined richness. You can achieve heights you never dreamt even existed before you started on your journey and find that you have talents never before revealed. The sense of success can be captivating but not in a self-satisfied way. As a life-long and active learner, you will find that you develop humility as well as ability; knowing that there is always more to learn. Life will never be dull. There will always be something to intrigue and fascinate you. You will find that your interest in other people will expand and finding out how they tick will provide greater insight. Every day will dawn full of promise and you will never be disappointed because your abilities to reflect and consider will ensure that there will be something, even a minor event, on which to ponder.

The interaction of the different factors in our universe changes our situation. Reg Revans, the father of Action Learning, said:

Learning must be equal to or greater than the rate of change.[9]

If learning is slower the result is slow decay and ultimately death, as the dinosaur discovered. It is better in the long run, therefore, to learn. Learning is life. The human form continues to survive because people are able to adapt. Adapting requires the current situation to be weighed up and considered. The latent threats must be spotted and the risks inherent must be identified accurately. Opportunities are sensed and possible options considered. On the basis of the analysis, decisions are made and then action taken. Usually the decision involves a different or new thought or option being formed and the resultant action leads to some form of change to the situation. This is learning being applied. Learning does not need to be revolutionary. Evolution does very nicely, as a few hundred centuries of human growth have proven.

---

[9] Revans, R, *The Origin and Growth of Action Learning* (Bromley: Chartwell Bratt) 1985.

Chapter 2

What Influences Learning?

INTRODUCTION

In the first chapter we discussed the definition of learning and touched on the difference between process and outcomes. Reference was made to the conditions required to support learning from a theoretic point of view to start building the foundation on which to develop our understanding. This will help to improve your own learning and that of those whose learning you may support. This chapter will move on to examine the needs of the individual learner. We will begin by exploring how individuals initially learn what they are able to do as fully functioning adults. This will provide the platform from which we can review the factors that have contributed to the creation of an individual's self-image and current body of knowledge. We will then be in a position to identify what action might be taken to exploit the opportunities for learning that exist around us all of the time.

WE MAKE CHOICES

The first thing to recognise is our ability to decide. We are free in more ways than we may believe to make choices about what we do and the way we live our lives. One of the main distinguishing differences between human beings and animals is our ability to make choices about how to behave. We control the way we can respond to situations and to other people; we do not have to react without thought. We have the intellectual ability to consider options and alternatives unlike animals that react to stimuli – though watching some people may lead you to think otherwise! Our decisions, however, are not unlimited. We are constrained and bounded by a number of factors. These factors exist around us and are part of us.

Our understanding of these factors develops as we progress through the stages of maturation and youthful education. As William

Wordsworth said in *Intimations from Immortality*[1]:

> Shades of the prison house begin to close
> Upon the growing Boy ...
> Behold the Child among his new-born blisses,
> A six years' Darling of a pigmy size!
> See, where 'mid work of his own hand he lies,
> Fretted by sallies of his mother's kisses
> With light upon him from his father's eyes!
> See, at his feet, some little plan or chart,
> Some fragment from his dream of human life,
> Shaped by himself with newly-learned art;
> A wedding or a festival,
> A mourning or a funeral;
> And this hath now his heart,
> And unto this he frames his song:
> Then will he fit his tongue
> To dialogues of business, love, strife;
> But it will not be long
> Ere this will be thrown aside,
> And with new joy and pride
> The little Actor cons another part;
> Filling from time to time his "humorous stage"
> With all the Persons, down to palsied Age,
> That Life brings with her in her equipage;
> As if his whole vocation
> Were endless imitation.

The prison-house walls bound our view of what we believe is possible and what we believe we are able to do. Some of the walls are real. Society imposes constraints on us through laws and regulations that control what we are permitted or forbidden to do. But some of the walls are not as fixed as we think them to be. Admittedly, our freedoms and rights cease as soon as they begin to impact on other people but we do have the ability to negotiate these boundaries. Sometimes we

---

[1] Wordsworth, W, "Intimations of Immortality" from *Recollections of Early Childhood* in Wordsworth Poetic Works (ed. T Hutchinson, revised by E de Selincourt) (Oxford: OUP) 1969.

erect walls to suit our own purposes or to fit with a view of the world which is comfortable or convenient.

WALLS AROUND OUR LEARNING

The walls may not be either as near or as solid as we think they are or want them to be. We develop an image of ourselves in relation to other people and the world in which we live as we grow in experience and increase our knowledge. This understanding is based partly on fact and partly on the reality that has been constructed by us and for us. This second reality is a combination of fixed points and shifting holograms. The holograms are the fictions we always have believed but are not totally sure about.

Take the example of the middle-aged woman who was convinced she could not ride a bicycle. As a child her parents could not afford to buy her or her brother push bikes and as none of their friends had bikes, there was never the chance for her to try. As she grew older she realised that her sense of balance was not that good and in any case riding bikes simply did not fit with her life style and self-image. In her own view she could not ride a bike and did not even want to try. At least until she became involved with a group of people who could ride bikes. They decided they wanted to have a day out on one of the new cycleways. Our friend was faced with a dilemma: change her self-image and learn how to ride a bike or miss out on a shared activity. She learnt how to cycle in a surprisingly short time.

It is not easy for adults to learn new skills or acquire new knowledge. Most of the time we remain bounded by our view of the world and our self-image. We know who we are, what we can and cannot do and what is likely to happen in our everyday lives. Making changes to the walls that surround us can be difficult: we have to admit that there are flaws or shortcomings, deficiencies or gaps. This admission can be seen as one of weakness. It is not so; it is one that takes courage. Understanding that the walls are not fixed or rigid lets you accept that gaps in your knowledge and skills are not flaws; they exist simply because you have not had the chance to acquire them – yet. But filling these gaps may mean that you have to let go of your current view of reality and open your mind to the possibility of another.

Before we look at how to test the reality of the walls, let us spend a little more time examining how they are constructed in the first place. They are products of our exposure to ideas and possibilities, other people, our own personality and our experiences.

Figure 2.1: Walls Around our Learning

Our exposure to ideas and possibilities

Experience

Other people

Personality – motivation and learning style

LEARNING FROM EXPERIENCE

We described in chapter 1 how concrete experience is the starting point of Kolb's Learning Cycle. We know the importance of learning from experience and the value of putting theoretical knowledge into practice. We talk of learning at the University of Life and recognise the worth of experienced, practised and competent staff yet we find it difficult to recognise and credit this form of learning.

Mumford gives three different types of experience from which you might learn:

1. when you are faced with new demands – for example when you move into a new area of work or into a new role

2. when you are faced with a new type of situation or event – for example when visiting other work places or dealing with new customers

3. when doing your everyday job.[2]

The last is perhaps the hardest type of experience to recognise as a learning occasion. One reason for this is that it happens all of the time, without us noticing that anything special is occurring. This is because learning from experience is the first type of learning in which we are engaged. It starts at birth. Experiential learning is natural and normal. So much so, that for most of the time we do not know what is going on.

Most of the events that happen every day are simply more of the same. We pass through our daily routines on automatic pilot. Seldom does anything extraordinary take place. If extraordinary things did happen every day, they would be normal and so routine. Moreover, we would not be able to cope with the variety and the mental demands, for the human brain is inherently lazy. It looks for short cuts and simple rules of thumb so that it can avoid work. It learns tricks and systems to enable it to predict what is likely to happen by codifying previous learning and building constructs. Reference was made to these in chapter 1.

Unfortunately this mental laziness leads to errors and biases. Research has shown that novices are more efficient than experts because they use checklists and other tools to ensure that the steps they need to follow are made explicit. This is to make sure they do not forget anything as they are learning and practising. Experts, as a result of their experience and learning, develop a structure of knowledge linked by shortcuts and *aide-mémoires*. This avoids the need to go from basic principals for every event they have to deal with. They are able to rely on their memory and draw on the body of knowledge built up from their initial training and extended with experience and hopefully continued professional development (CPD).

However, without reference to the checklists, the experts can forget certain elements, especially when faced with aspects of the job that do not occur very often. They can also become blinded by their

---

[2] Mumford, A, *How Managers can Develop Managers* (Aldershot: Gower) 1993.

own knowledge. Believing themselves to be expert, they can find it hard to admit to their own lack of knowledge. They find themselves travelling along narrow tramlines, following well-known patterns of thought. They may be unaware of knowledge and skills that exist beyond the boundaries of their expertise. When faced with a new problem the tendency is to try to solve it using existing methods and previous answers. The brain refuses to acknowledge the novelty and, therefore, can produce inappropriate solutions.

We saw in chapter 1 how the disparate disciplines have developed different understandings of learning. Of course they are all right and extremely well founded, based on thorough and respected research and insights. However, blindness to the offerings of other professions can limit one's ability to extend knowledge, understanding and skill and so constrain an individual's ability to learn from new experiences. If you do not recognise the newness in what on the surface may seem to be an ordinary event, you are not able to start the learning cycle. Even events which are repeats of previous ones can provide the opportunity to reflect on what you do and how you do it, especially if you have not thought about them like that before.

Any learning that results from this form of experience, if it is not made explicit, can be stored in the subconscious in ways that mean you are not aware of what you have learnt. The mental recording process in this case is a little like a video, recording automatically from the TV. If you do not keep an eye on the tape index, you cannot be certain that anything is being captured.

Learning from experiences is difficult to log. Events happen all the time. Which do you treat as being significant or outstanding? Which, after the passage of time, when you look back, will be remarkable? The answer is you do not know at the outset. Mumford suggests four approaches to learning from experience:

1. the intuitive approach

2. the incidental approach

3. the retrospective approach

4. the prospective approach.

Understanding how these occur makes it easier to log the event and the outcome.

The *intuitive approach* implies that learning is an inevitable consequence of having an experience. While the incident or event can be recalled in detail, the individual has some difficulty describing what was learnt or how the learning was achieved. Intuitive people tend to describe themselves as being Lifelong Learners but cannot say what learning activities they undertake. They benefit from the help of other people to help them reflect on the experience and abstract the learning.

The *incidental approach* (not to be confused with incidental learning) occurs when something jolts an individual from the normal routine. Perhaps something goes wrong or an unexpected event occurs. They mull over what has happened or even talk it through with a friend but they do not make any systematic analysis. They use hindsight to justify the way they behaved and possibly rationalise or explain away their reaction. They may vow not to do the same thing again or let other people put them into that sort of situation but they do not draw out learning points that can be applied to other situations. Again, the help of another, perhaps as mentor, may prove useful.

The *retrospective approach* is similar to the incidental approach in that an unexpected event provides the spur for review and abstraction of conclusions. In addition, people using the retrospective approach make use of routine events and engage in a more systematic analysis by using purposeful reflection, discussion and recording of the main points to come from the experience. The use of some tool to record the learning (for example a diary or log) may be helpful.

The *prospective approach* adds another dimension to the above. As well as engaging in review, the prospective learner plans how to abstract the learning *before* the event happens. While some events cannot be predicted, the prospective learner is aware of the chance that something *might* happen. Thus they are open to the possibility of learning and know how to capture the learning that results from experience.

The following model extends Kolb's Learning Cycle, which we discussed in chapter 1, to portray, simply, how the mental storing process occurs. The aim is to ensure that the experience is logged in the memory store and combined with previous learning so that it augments what is already known and is comprehended in a way that enables it to be accessed and used in the future.

Figure 2.2: Mental Storing Process

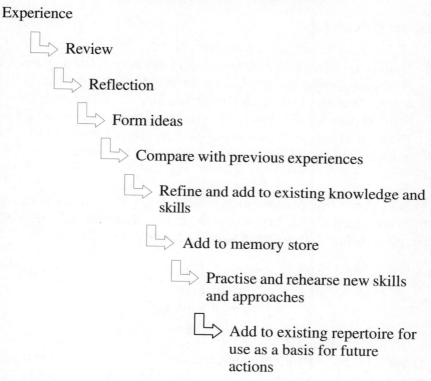

Experience

⤷ Review

⤷ Reflection

⤷ Form ideas

⤷ Compare with previous experiences

⤷ Refine and add to existing knowledge and skills

⤷ Add to memory store

⤷ Practise and rehearse new skills and approaches

⤷ Add to existing repertoire for use as a basis for future actions

One of the big challenges for educationalists is to find effective and simple ways of enabling people to make explicit the learning they have achieved from experience. So far, most of the ways, for example the Accreditation of Prior Experience and Learning (APEL) systems and the portfolios used for the certification of competence for the award of NVQs, can appear to be excessively bureaucratic. Their compilation can be time consuming without necessarily contributing to learning anything other than how to compile portfolios. This is an area where further research and the development of good practice would be enormously beneficial, especially if targets, resources and funding are tied to the achievement of certifiable outcomes and the award of qualifications.

LEARNING FROM OTHER PEOPLE

Direct influence

> *A father was seen in a café showing a baby how to use a spoon. He mimed feeding himself several times before giving the spoon to the infant who copied his parent's actions. It is likely that the baby did not know he was doing anything related to satiating his hunger, but he quickly had grasped the manual skills involved in lifting the empty spoon and putting it to his mouth.*

This example brings to mind two important points about learning from other people. The first is the role demonstration plays in helping people develop skills as the following nursery rhyme shows:

I do it normal
You do it slow
You do it with me
Off you go

The second and possibly the more important is the contribution made by role models. Role models are different to mentors. More of the latter presently. A role model may be a good or a negative influence on the learner. We have role models, as in the example of the father and the spoon, from our very earliest days. Obviously the first such models come from our immediate family and those closely involved with the home such as relatives, family friends and neighbours. As we grow older our circle of "influential others" expands to include school teachers, school friends, their siblings and parents, other school peers and the people involved in our and our family's lives. These people interact with us and with the other people around us. Sometimes we are central to the "play", other times we are merely members of the supporting cast, on occasions we are not even remotely involved in the action, just witnesses.

As we move away from our family, this circle of influence alters. Some people remain constant, new people join the circle, others leave and some come and go. The influence some of the people have over you will be helpful. They will contribute to your development in positive ways. They will introduce you to ideas, they will challenge you in supportive ways and provide useful feedback. You may not think of them in this light at the time. Remember the uncle who taught you how to ride your bike, his hand gently supportive in the small of your back until the second he gave you one big push. The push itself hurt, the shock of being propelled into independence was both scary and thrilling. The words used to describe your uncle at the moment would not necessarily be complimentary, if you had the time to think about them.

The influence other people have over your development may not be so supportive. These are the people who motivate you to achieve in spite of them. They are also the people who express ideas you think are repellent or simply wrong. They are the people whose behaviour you think is inexcusable, never to be replicated.

A useful exercise, called *significant other analysis*, can help you identify who has had the most influence on your development. The following diagram will help you name those whose influence has been positive, those whose impact has resulted in your choosing which patterns of behaviour or ideas to accept, replicate, adapt or reject.

Figure 2.3: Significant Other Analysis

Positive   Negative

Constant influence but not significant

Important at the time but not life changing

Significant influence

Direct, enduring influence

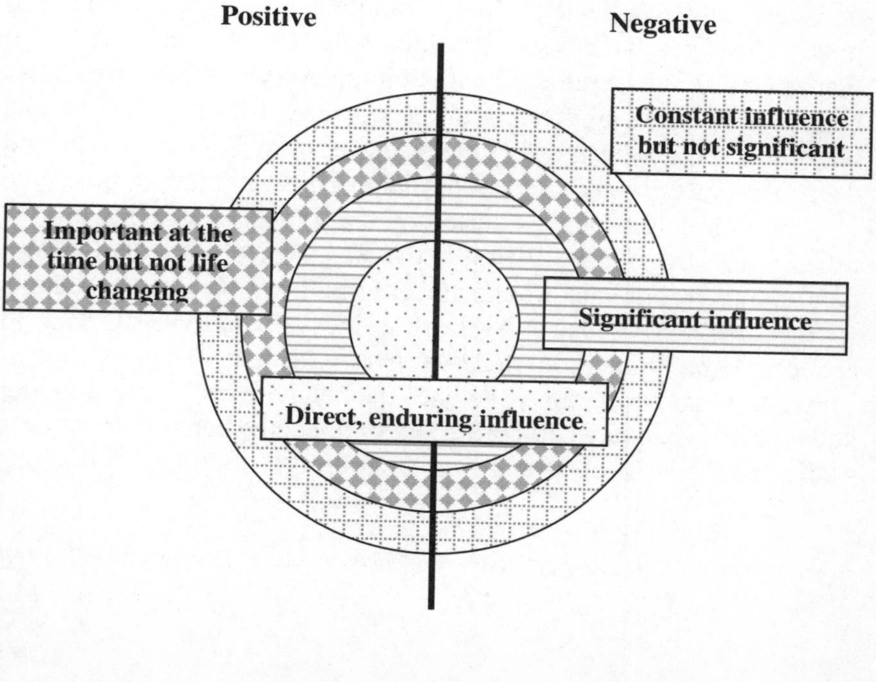

Indirect influence

Other people influence our behaviour and attitudes in many other ways in addition to the direct contact outlined above. This influence can be exercised through media such as television, radio and publications, for as we become more exposed to the wider world we become more receptive to other ideas and role models. In the transition from child to adulthood we begin to make up our own minds about which ideas to adopt and how to act. Remember the influences on you as you went through your teenage and early adult years? Some of the behaviours and attitudes you chose possibly were in direct conflict with those of your parents and significant others. Were they espoused as challenges to some of the deeper values these influential people were trying to instil in you?

You would also have been prey to advertising and propaganda designed to guide your behaviour and attitudes in a particular direction. Some messages will have been contained in pop songs, popular films, books and, increasingly, material available on the worldwide web. We live in a world full of information and ideas, all of which can influence our opinions and shape our views. Understanding where they come from and how they are formed is important, for our views influence how we act in certain situations. As we gain in experience and are exposed to more and more ideas, we begin to discriminate between them. We decide which to adopt as our own and which to reject. However, we are still shackled by our background. It is rare that a person enters adulthood with opinions very different from other people in their social group and background. Many of the lessons learnt will have occurred very early in life and will have been buried deep in the subconscious, as some will have been learned subliminally.

The indirect influence exerted by the society in which we grew up is very strong and difficult to resist. We are socialised and conditioned by our background and environment. Bandura called this *social learning.*[3] In his theory, he describes how individuals learn to replicate behaviours modelled by others. This happens in two ways. The individual deliberately watches the behaviour of the role model and is able to decide whether to adopt or reject the behaviour patterns witnessed. This form of learning is common, often called demon-

---

[3] Bandura, A, *Social Learning Theory* (Englewood Cliffs N.J.: Prentice-Hall) 1977.

stration or instruction. The role model is usually a more experienced worker or teacher. The learner is shown a set of actions and if the instructor is competent, information is given to explain why the actions are carried out in that particular way.

The other way we replicate behaviours is more insidious. We watch people all of the time, starting from the time we first become aware of what is going on around us, as the example of parent and child on page 28 illustrates. We see which kinds of actions work in different situations and which do not. We see what leads our friends into trouble at school and we hear people talking in the local shop, and we remember. We do not necessarily know that we are listening, watching and remembering but the images and ideas get logged in the recesses of our memory.

We are also affected by the subtle systems of rewards and punishments that are built into our culture. Images of "successful people" are held up as exemplars to be copied, as their life style is to be aspired to. There are also images of what happens to those who do not conform to approved patterns of behaviour. We are shaped and moulded by these pressures and images of which ideas and behaviours are to be followed and those to be avoided.

Even when we think that we are mature, self-determining adults capable of making up our own minds, we are still bounded by our society's cultural mores. Sometimes we do not know of these until someone whose background is different to our own brings them into our consciousness. Religion provides a good example of how deep these mores can lie. We tend to think that, in Western Europe, we live in a sceptical, free-thinking society, tolerant of a wide range of views. Yet the influence of the various branches of the Christian Church is deeply entrenched in many aspects of our society and underpins many of our everyday rituals and routines. For example people who would never dream of going to celebrate communion believe that a "proper" marriage ceremony is held in church. Until a different set of values is proffered, we tend not to question traditional customs.

Many of the very deep-seated beliefs and patterns of behaviour have developed over many years and are shared by the majority of the society's members. Because so many of us share the same assumptions, we rarely have any need to question or even explore them. The people that do tend to be seen as rebels, mavericks or philosophers. As we do not often think about these beliefs we take them for granted, assume that everyone else shares them and seldom discuss them.

Garfinkel, an American sociologist, put this to the test.[4] The report of his experiment describes how a number of students were asked to act like lodgers in their own homes. But other members of the family were not informed as the experiment had been devised to explore their reactions. Imagine the confusion this sudden role change caused!

Discussion is the key to understanding belief systems and reasons for behaviour. As our value systems and shared assumptions are manifested in our behaviour, knowing what we think, and why, is essential if we are to gain insight into how our own and other peoples' learning processes operate. For what we do illustrates what we think; what we say outlines what we believe. These two sentences are not always true, for we are able to control how we behave and what we say. But most often we act without any deep thought and speak with little consideration of the content.

The attempts made during the Second World War to persuade housewives to use dried egg contains an important lesson. There was a great reluctance to use the yellow powder, yet fresh eggs were simply not available. Exhortation was failing so a series of public recipe demonstrations was organised. It was found that if members of the audience *publicly* committed themselves to using the substitute, the chances of continuing use were increased. Subsequent research explained that this happened because of a need for our attitudes and behaviour to be in harmony; otherwise we suffer from *cognitive dissonance.*

Our attitudes are captured and codified in language. The words we learn and our understanding of their meaning are stored and the ones most frequently used form our operational vocabulary. The way we use these words – how we construct sentences – and the way we speak are also a result of learning. All are capable of change. It was not just Professor Higgins and Eliza who engaged in manipulating speech in order to bring about behaviour changes, which in turn altered the way Eliza was perceived.

---

4 Garfinkel, H, (reported in Chapter 6) "Society as Process" in Cashmore, E & B Mullan, *Approaching Social Theory* (London: Heinemann) 1983, pp. 114–116.

Cashmore and Mullan, in defining social research, say:

> We learn to acquire, convey, retain and sometimes change socially recognised meanings about all sorts of things through, at first, being talked to and then talking back. The meanings of things are brought home to use by our parents and others talking about them. So the complex meanings we give to things are shaped through language . . . When we pick up the threads of language and begin to use them, we acquire the ability to store meanings and project into the future on the basis of those meanings. Present experiences can be related to past ones, which can be summoned into consciousness by the use of words. Future experiences can be anticipated and planned for.[5]

As we move into groups other than our family circle we acquire words and patterns of speech particular to each different and distinct group to which we belong. We learn what type of speech is acceptable at home, what is acceptable in the classroom, what is allowed in the playground and what is not. The subtleties underlying the differences are quite difficult to explain, which is one reason why learning English as a second language is not easy. As we move into wider circles the number of different types of language multiplies. Our working life is characterised by the use of what is called, pejoratively, jargon – words developed uniquely for a particular use. (For example in Birmingham libraries the bookshelves were called "presses", a term dating back to the early days of storing books and manuscripts. In Rotherham libraries, no one had ever heard of the word.) Our social life is described by slang and, with friends and colleagues, we have a system of codes and shorthand terms to describe our shared values and assumptions. We all know what we mean – or do we? Do we give other people a false impression? Are we capable of explaining to people who are not in the know? Do we know why we use the words we do and where they came from? Do they convey value systems and experiences that are no longer relevant?

Cashmore goes on to say:

> The capacity for reflection ... comes with the acquisition of

---

5 Cashmore, E & B Mullan, *Approaching Social Theory* (London: Heinemann) 1983.

language; without using words it would be impossible to think back or ahead. Furthermore it is through reflection that we become conscious not only of the world about us but of ourselves; we become self-conscious – and this is critically important ... if we are to understand the way in which we learn and influence the learning of others. What we say to other people tells them what is important and not important, how to act and what not to do. Most importantly it influences what they think. The power of social learning and the place occupied by role models must not be under valued.[6]

Role models are people who occupy an important position in a group or society. They may be social leaders and are held up as examples by and to others. Their behaviour is observed and their speech heard. They may be seen as people whose ideas, behaviour and speech are to be adopted. They can range from cult figures, such as pop stars, TV and film celebrities and other popular figures, to neighbours. The power of their influence can be seen, for example, in the way David Beckham's haircut has affected the income of male hairdressers across the country. The "Take your Daughters to Work" initiative exposes young women to other people at work to influence their perception of what might be possible and what they might achieve.

Models of what not to do are also held up to help people learn. We use derogative terms to describe people whose behaviour and ideas are not socially acceptable. Sometimes the result of this is to create anti-heroes but more often those people are shunned and rejected. Groups are stereotyped and are allocated a position in the social class system. Tax inspectors, for example, do not necessarily occupy a role in the public psyche that most people aspire to share.

Role models, who occupy powerful positions in society and groups, are able to determine the sort of behaviour, language and ideas which are the "approved" ones by a system of rewards and punishments and the exercise of their power. Often the dynamics of this are not obvious and individuals are not aware of the processes that are happening around them. So they learn unconsciously to copy the behaviour of the role model. Sometimes role models may not appreciate the influence they have on others.

---

[6] *Ibid.*

This use of social learning can be seen in the processes used by groups to ensure that new members learn how to conform to the group's existing values and take on preferred patterns of behaviour. The research conducted by Mayo and others in the Hawthorne Studies was the first time this was described.[7] It was found that work groups set down acceptable levels of production. Each person was paid at piece rates according to their individual output. Anyone who exceeded the group level was called a *"Rate buster"*, anyone failing to meet the standard was known as a *"Chiseller"*. This demonstrates how derogatory language is used to punish non-conformists. The nature of the relationships with supervisors was also described. No matter how much the individual supervisor may be liked outside work, inside, the role-holder was always the enemy, not party to group in-jokes nor included in social activities.

Social learning is put to work to ensure that new workers are quickly and thoroughly accepted by their new colleagues and fitted in to the organisation as a whole. Good quality induction programmes acknowledge its potential and use its benefits. They have an underpinning structure that ensures a new person is given the information needed to understand the basic value systems and assumptions (for example the organisation's history and mission are explained) and that they are exposed early to "approved" role models. Some organisations formalise the role model by attaching new starters to experienced and well-regarded employees in "buddying" or "mentoring" schemes. The experienced employee is there to guide, inform and support the new person during their initial weeks and to provide "openings" to the organisation's informal society. These people are able to ease the new starter's way in and help them avoid the sort of social gaffs the uninitiated can easily make. Likewise they are able to protect the new person from some of the initiation ceremonies and jokes that still can be found in organisations.

Thus in a well-structured induction programme a new person is able to learn and understand the value systems of their new employer and the sub-groups that make it up. They learn the meaning of the jargon and how the basic systems operate. They know what is expected of them in their new job and understand the contribution they will make to the achievement of their employer's objectives. They will

---

[7] Mayo, E, *The Social Problems of an Industrial Civilisation* (Boston: Harvard) 1945.

understand how the formal communications systems work and which parts of the grapevine to trust and which to doubt. They will quickly learn who are the social leaders and who to be wary of. They will learn which patterns of behaviour to copy and which to avoid if they want to be successful in the organisation. Without this form of help, some people are never able to learn all the subtleties that make up the organisation in which they work.

SELF-LEARNING

As we develop and mature we gain in understanding. We learn who we are and what we are in relation to others. We obtain information about ourselves from reflection and from the results of the actions we take. We also receive feedback from others. Feedback is the information we are given about ourselves by other people, sometimes uncanvassed and sometimes unwarranted. Our families provide information about our background and our genetic make-up. "Oh!" screams a grandmother in delight. "Your father did just the same thing at your age". Information, irritating as it may be, forms, socialises and constrains us. Are we products of our genetic make-up, pre-programmed to follow the family line? Are we empty vessels, born ready to absorb new ideas and learn our own abilities as we progress through life? Or perhaps both?

Such deep philosophical discussions cannot be concluded within the scope of a small book such as this. But anyone interested in the learning progress needs to be aware of these issues and how genetic make-up and personality as well as environment contribute and constrain an individual's readiness and ability to learn.

Personality

What is personality, how best to describe it, how best to define it and how best to measure it? These issues have concerned psychologists for over a century. Distinct schools of thought and ways of portraying personality have been developed to answer these questions. Perhaps the three most often found in the context of employment are those of Jung, Cattel (whose 16 personality factors were the basis of the OPQ test) and Myers-Briggs. There are others. They and the numerous variations have been developed and are often found in personality questionnaires used as a means of assessing applicants during recruitment and selection. These and other forms of intelligence tests are described by Hayes and Orrell.[8] Without getting into the complexity of this, for the purposes of this text, let us simply say that personality is at the centre of an individual's uniqueness.

The formation of personality and its component structure is not a simple matter. We have already discussed the effect significant others have on our early development and learning and the way we are conditioned by the society and groups in which we exist. Our experiences and the lessons to which we are exposed add layer upon layer to the patina that surrounds the rich, complex being that is an adult.

Sometimes this is said to be like an onion. But unlike an onion the layers are made up of material more complex than skins with different degrees of desiccation. And at the heart of the personality is a core very unlike the other layers and far more difficult to define. Even an individual has difficulty in knowing her or his total self. The Johari Window is a simple model that neatly illustrates levels of self-knowledge.

Figure 2.4: The Johari Window

Self

		Things I know about me	Things I do not know about me
Others	Things other people know about me	*The Arena*	*The Blind Spot*
	Things other people do not know about me	*The Façade*	*Totally Unknown*

8 Hayes, N & S Orrell, *Psychology: An Introduction* (Harlow: Addison Wesley Longman) 1998.

Increased self-awareness is achieved by reducing the size of the lower right quadrant. This is done by obtaining feedback from others and reflecting on your experience. As you learn more about yourself, the central line is pushed towards the right and to the bottom of the Window. Thus *The Arena,* the public part of your personality, is enlarged. The more you understand yourself and obtain useful feedback, the less likely it is that you present a false *Façade* to other people. You will have fewer *Blind Spots,* those parts of you which everyone else knows about but even your best friend will not tell you, and the area which is *Totally Unknown* to everyone, even to you, will be smaller.

However, pushing back the lines is not easy and it is probable that no one has total knowledge of themselves. There is always a chance that the way you respond to a new situation or challenge will surprise you. One reason why we have such difficulty in achieving total self-knowledge is because we are products of the genes we inherit from our parents, which are melded in unique combinations so that even identical twins are different. A very simple illustration of the multiplicity of influences that work together, in harmony and conflict, to shape each individual can be seen in Figure 2.5.

Figure 2.5: Influencing Factors

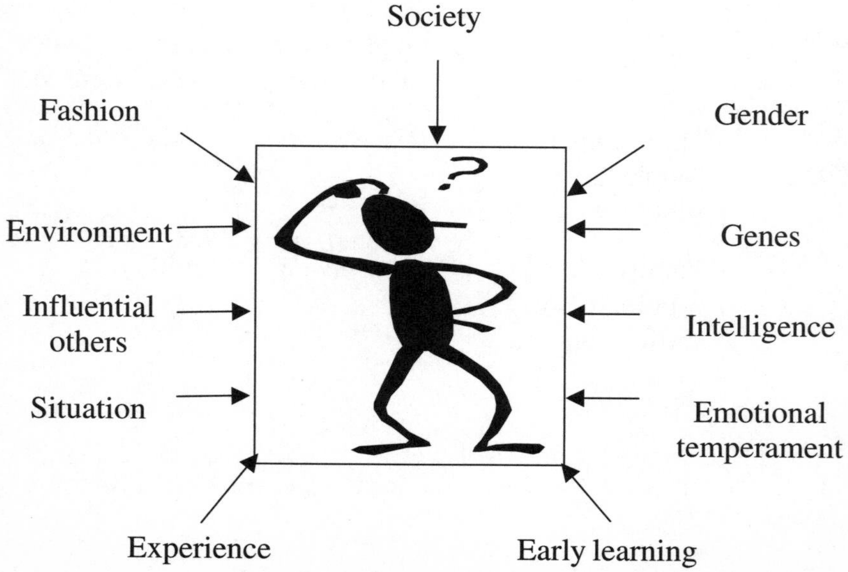

Society

Fashion   Gender

Environment   Genes

Influential
others   Intelligence

Situation   Emotional
                                                temperament

Experience   Early learning

Clearly some of these will interact with each other and moderate the sort of impact they have on any one individual. The interaction will change depending on the combination of people involved, the situation, the time and other external forces. The external factors will be affected by the way the individual responds to them in turn. Some theories maintain that the underpinning components of an individual's personality are already formed by a very young age. Others recognise that we change and develop as we go through different experiences.

Understanding what these forces are and how they influence you will assist you to identify the types of events, activities and aids that help you learn. The more you know about how you learn and the more able a learner you become, the more able you will be to determine and influence your own destiny. You will be less likely to be a victim of circumstances and will be better equipped to deal with new situations and people.

Readiness for learning

Governing your ability to learn will be your degree of readiness and your preparedness to respond to new ideas and events. These will be influenced partly by your personality and partly by your free will. We accepted earlier that one of the distinctive features of the human being is the ability to make choices, but those choices are bounded by a number of constraints. Some of these spring from external forces and influences but some are part of the idiosyncratic personality. We may appear to be at liberty to accept or reject new ideas and appear to have choices in the matter. However, our capacity to make decisions is limited by our mental abilities. Whether these are fixed or whether they can be learnt and developed is an interesting debate, very similar to that concerning the nature of personality. It is the "nurture-nature" debate. The critical factor is to identify which aspects of your make-up are fixed and which can be changed.

Intelligence

Attempts to measure intelligence were started at the end of the nineteenth and beginning of the twentieth centuries. Galton and Binet, as described by Hayes and Orrell,[9] are credited with the early work

---

[9] *Ibid.*

and their efforts have provided the foundations for much of what has followed. Their ideas presented some ethical difficulties which have not yet been totally resolved. One of the main issues is whether those with higher levels of intelligence should receive special treatment and those with the lowest be regarded as "subnormal".

Clearly the central issue in the debate is, what constitutes intelligence? Hayes and Orrell state:

> We wouldn't argue that everyone was exactly the same. It seems clear that there are individual differences and that people have different cognitive styles which mean that they take to some kinds of learning more readily than others ... One of the arguments which psychologists have about intelligence is whether the single thing called intelligence exists at all.[10]

To answer this question and see how it applies to learning we must look at the measures of intelligence in general use. The first of these, most commonly applied, is the sort of intelligence needed to be successful in the achievement of academic qualifications.

Qualifications are sought on application forms and their attainment is regarded as a measure of general intellect as well as educational ability. Unfortunately, standards, names and assessment systems have changed to such an extent that many employers are confused and find it difficult to make accurate assessments, as it is not always clear exactly what the qualifications signify. Moreover, it has long been recognised that some people who do not achieve academically nevertheless have abilities that are worthwhile, valuable and, in some cases, scarce. In chapter 1 we discussed how the National Vocational Qualification system had been established in an attempt to accredit abilities in more work-related ways and to provide a structure in which the different awards could be harmonised and their levels compared.

Other ways of assessing intelligence have also been developed. Binet's early tests were in the form of everyday tasks that a child was expected to be able to complete at a given age. This idea was used to create a way of quantifying mental ability, so if a child is able to complete a task typical of a child younger or older, the first child is assigned the second child's age. The mental age is then divided by the

---

[10] *Ibid.*

child's actual age and multiplied by 100 to produce the child's IQ (intelligence quota). IQ is widely used as a reflection of an individual's intellectual ability for children and adults. However, Hayes and Orrell state:

> One problem with using age to calculate IQ scores is that adult mental development is very much more variable [than that of children]. Although some adults continue to increase their IQs throughout their lives, others show a decline as they get older. (It seems to have everything to do with practice – people who continue to learn and are open-minded in seeking out new information increase their IQs, others seem to let their "mental muscles" atrophy through disuse.)[11]

Though they were popular at one time, general intelligence tests are less frequently used for occupational purposes and have been replaced by more specific tests of mental ability. The use of *cognitive ability tests* is based on the belief that, in addition to general intelligence, there are a number of specific skills, such as verbal fluency and critical reasoning, that indicate intellect. These tests are used individually or in batteries to explore a range of abilities. But like Binet's tests, they rely on variation from the norm and the use of comparisons with a sample population to determine ability.

Efforts are constantly being made by test publishers to increase the link between the theoretical definitions of intelligence and the mental skills sought for employment. They are also trying to ensure that the tests are free from unfair bias. Checks are made to compare and contrast results obtained by men and women, and those from different ethnic groups. It is very difficult to assess whether these factors are at play once any obvious bias has been eliminated and despite extensive efforts there remains some concern that they may discriminate unfairly.

Some of the commercial test publishers supply intelligence tests for use in connection with selection and other forms of assessment. Weschsler Adult Intelligence scale is a typical example. This test examines memory, comprehension, letter–number sequencing, arithmetic, matrix reasoning, digit span and digital symbol coding,

---

[11] *Ibid.*

similarities, information processing, picture arrangement and completion, vocabulary and block design. The other cognitive ability tests explore specific aptitudes such as verbal and spatial reasoning, critical thinking and certain occupational skills such as organising information, numeracy and mechanical skills.

The sheer range of different categories listed above begins to illustrate the difficulty encountered in defining and measuring intelligence. Hayes and Orrell describe the work of Sternberg, who drew attention to the very different nature of the separate types of intelligence in a way that suggests that different kinds of job need very different mental abilities.[12] But it is not always easy to compare them and assign value to their worth. Decide, for example, between the intelligence of the surgeon waiting to conduct an operation and the knowledge of the cleaner who needs to ensure the environment and equipment are sterile. We tend, sadly, to create a hierarchy that places academic learning at the top and other forms of intellectual ability lower down and to make pejorative judgements about them.

One area of intelligence that has been sorely neglected is that concerned with the ability to learn. If you are able to understand how you learn best and recognise where your strengths and weaknesses lie, you will be far better equipped to continue to learn and adjust to new circumstances than the person who has little insight and limited learning skills.

Creativity

The ability to create something totally new is generally regarded as a special type of intelligence. A critical question is whether we all have that ability innately but, for whatever reason, some of us stop using it. Others argue that it is a distinct form of intelligence and present in only some people. Regardless of the answer, it is true to say that some people are not able to generate new thoughts or ideas; they remain within the bounds of their existing knowledge and skills. Rather than providing the answer, it is more important here to consider whether it is possible to learn how to be creative.

Some maintain that creativity is an aspect of problem solving and we know that problem-solving skills are becoming increasingly

---

[12] *Ibid.*

important at work as more decisions are devolved to front line staff. It is widely accepted that people are able to improve their problem-solving skills by learning techniques and using frameworks. Techniques such as lateral thinking and "thinking outside the box" are well known and used extensively. Some would argue that similar approaches can be used for the development of creative thinking skills; others, however, maintain that creativity is part of personality: you either have it or you do not.

The ability to be creative does not link automatically to artistic abilities. They are two distinct areas of competency which may often be found in one person. They can also exist equally well apart. Creativity relates to how well an individual is able to operate at the boundaries of their knowledge. It describes their inclination and ability to go beyond the limits of their preference for remaining within the confines of the known.

For those people who are not easy about stepping outside their zones of comfort, the ways in which they return to learning and how well they are supported are critical. In the early stages, it is vital that they are able to see their way back to the known. If they are left stranded in an unknown, unfamiliar situation, the responses most likely to be generated will be of panic or flight rather than learning. However, if they are helped, guided and allowed to feel "safe" as they engage in the journey, they will be likely to continue.

Risk taking

An individual's willingness to take risks is not too dissimilar from creativity. Some people by nature and/or experience are averse to taking risks. They do not gamble, nor do they speculate. They view change as a challenging venture whose outcome is uncertain and the amount of effort required to undertake the venture as far higher than the value of any possible outcome. This of course assumes the outcome is positive. There is a good chance of its not being so. They understand the curse "May you live in interesting times".

Those who relish risk see the chances of obtaining an outcome that is different to the status quo worth the required investment, for to them any outcome is better than staying the same. They believe that this is not an option. They accept, in a dynamic world, that other influences outside their direct control but having a direct effect on them will affect choices, possible behaviours and even ideas. To their mind, it is more beneficial to take a positive approach to risk taking. This, they believe, will enable them to have more control over what is happening and increase the chances of their preferred outcome being achieved.

Two dimensions can be used to describe risk-taking inclinations in individuals: Innovators and Adapters. These very useful concepts can be used to identify on which side of the fence you sit and your inclination to make changes. When asked, however, there is a chance that you will reply, "It depends". Your response to whether you are inclined to take risk depends very much on your assessment of the situation and chance of obtaining a favourable outcome. It also depends on how the risk is presented to you.

Research, for example that carried out by Kahneman and Tversky,[13] into decision making has found that our decisions depend on our starting point and whether we are facing the potential of gains or losses. We tend to be more cautious when we are in the domain of gain, preferring a certain outcome with lower value returns rather than one that involves any risk, even if the desired outcome is worth more. However, if we are faced with loses, we prefer to take a great risk of losing rather than the certainty of losing less. It has also been found that we tend to over-weight the probability of events with a low chance of occurrence and under-weight the probability of events with a moderate-to-high likelihood of happening.

Thus when faced with choices, we do not necessarily act rationally in making our decisions. We take risks if we think we may lose and avoid them if there is a chance of winning. We prefer to conserve rather than gamble. Our assessment of the probability of events happening is also flawed. We think unlikely things might happen and the chances of likely things happening are few, as Pratchett jokingly said "Scientists have calculated that the chances ... are millions to one. But ... million-to-one chances happen nine times out of ten."[14]

How we assess the chance is affected by how the situation is presented to us – how it is framed. Thus how options are described, in terms of losing or winning outcomes, is known to influence

[13] Kahneman, D & A Tversky, "Choices, Values and Frames" in H R Arkes & K R Hammond *Judgement and Decision Making: An Interdisciplinary Reader* (Cambridge: Cambridge University Press) 1986.

[14] Pratchett, T, *Mort* (London: Victor Gollanz) 1987.

people's responses to the choices available to them. Generally the pain of losing something is perceived to be greater than the value of obtaining something, even when the worth of the two is actually the same.

The following example taken from Bazerman shows how choices can be influenced simply by the way in which they are framed.[15]

Imagine that the senior management board of a car factory is faced with severe economic difficulties. It seems as though there is no choice but to close three production lines and make 6,000 employees redundant. The production manager has put forward two plans:

Plan A   Will result in the closure of two of the production lines and loss of 4,000 jobs.
Plan B   Has a two-thirds chance of all three production lines being closed and all 6,000 jobs lost but has a one-third chance of losing none of the production lines and no jobs.

Which would you chose?
On the other hand, the trade union came forward with a pair of alternative plans:

Plan C   Will save one of the production lines and 2,000 jobs.
Plan D   Offers a one-third chance of saving all three production lines and all of the 6,000 jobs but there is the two-thirds chance that it will not save any of the jobs or production lines.

Which do you prefer?

Technically both sets of options are the same, yet trials found that most people (over 80 per cent) chose Plan C and Plan B. People preferred to *save* jobs rather than risk *losing* any. This little experiment bears out other research that found that people treat risks concerning

---

[15] Bazerman, M H, *Judgement in Managerial Decision Making* (New York: John Wiley & Co.) 1994.

gains differently from the way they approach risks concerning losses.

Understanding this is important when you consider how you approach opportunities for learning. If you are aware that the way the options are presented to you is likely to influence your decisions you will be better able to stand back from them. Assessing the situation in different ways will help you reframe it and consider a full range of options before making any final choices.

We tend to assume that learning is *a good thing* and that those reluctant to engage are foolish. This is neither fair nor accurate and does not give adequate recognition to those who approach learning with some trepidation. They may have had previous bad experiences of being involved in learning. (We must remember that the formal education system has failed to help a substantial number of people learn how to read and work with numbers.) The proportion of adults classified as being functionally illiterate stands at about one in six.

Learning is a risky business. It involves entering a new situation. The chances of a desirable outcome being achieved are uncertain. The price for engaging in learning may be high and the very process difficult. Moreover, the outcome may not, in any case, be desirable.

Learning results in more than qualifications, new knowledge and additional skills. The process involves an experience and change. You may not want to undergo that change and have that particular type of experience, especially if you have never done anything like that before. You might find yourself with a group of people the like of whom you have never encountered previously. You might become like them, adopt their ideas and replicate their behaviours. This may mean that you will end up different from the people you currently mix with. Then what will happen?

MOTIVATION TO LEARN

The reasons for engaging in learning are many. Sometimes people are given no choice and approach the opportunity with a large amount of misgiving. Some people enter with closed minds, determined to resist and reject new ideas. Most people are prepared to accept that they may get something from the experience, even if they are not sure what, or whether they actually want it. Later, we will look at the reasons why people learn. For the time being, let us explore in a little more depth the concept of motivation, so you will be able to identify what it is that drives you to take, or not take, a particular action at a particular time.

In the 1930's, Abraham Maslow conducted research into the factors that are believed to motivate or drive an individual to action.[16] He suggested that there was a five-level hierarchy; progression to the next level depended on the satisfaction of the level below. This hierarchy of needs is often used to describe motivation at work. Maslow did not intend it to be so limited. It applies equally well to other situations, particularly learning.

Figure 2.6: Abraham Maslow's Hierarchy of Needs

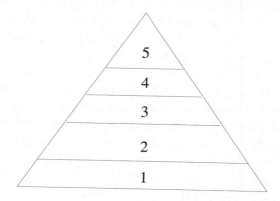

1. The first level contains the needs relating to *physical concerns* – food, safety, comfort – and we learn quickly how to maintain our bodily functions.

2. At the second level our needs relate to *shelter and security*. We strive to protect ourselves from harm and danger and find warm and dry places to sit and sleep.

3. The third level addresses our desires to *form relationships and operate in groups*. Early learning is known to involve the development of simple communication and social skills to equip

---

[16] Maslow, A, *Motivation and Personality* (New York: Harper) 1954.

us to do this. We need to belong to groups of people whose values and behaviour patterns we share.

4. To reach the fourth level, we seek and find *respect and approval* from members of those groups and of wider society. We present ourselves and behave in ways we think will result in a positive response from other people.

5. The fifth level, at the top of the hierarchy, is *self-actualisation*. This is the stage when we have realised our full potential. We are now capable of continued self-development and the full use of our creative abilities. We are able to apply these talents across the whole range of human endeavour to represent articulate, self-confident and truly assertive people. In this state we are not self-satisfied nor do we impose our will or opinions on others. You will find people operating at this level are modest about their achievements and more than willing to help others in their progression along the learning curve.

The idea of a progressive hierarchy has been doubted. There is plenty of evidence to undermine the idea of straight-line upward movement, for superficially it suggests that once a need at a lower level has been satisfied, the individual concerns themselves with obtaining satisfaction at the next. People are known to seek the gratification of lower level needs even when ones at a higher level have been amply fulfilled. Of course this is not always the case; it does not account for greed. Maslow's Hierarchy of Needs nevertheless provides a useful means of helping us understand that human beings will endeavour to ensure that their needs at all five levels are supplied and, if they are not, will make extra efforts to provide for the basic essential requirements.

The five needs also suggest areas where action can be taken to encourage individuals to make extra efforts. Some of this thinking has been used to underpin the design of reward systems such as payment by results schemes. Not only do they offer the chance of gaining extra money for extra effort, they contain the negative aspect. If you do not continue to perform to the level expected, you will receive less than before. Rewards and punishments have long been recognised as basic ways of influencing individual behaviours.

Maslow's motivators can also be used to help us identify what helps people learn. The drive to satisfy the next level of need clearly will encourage us to learn the skills and acquire the knowledge required to fulfil that need. But if it is under threat – will that motivate learning? There is a greater chance that the *fight/flight* response will be generated. We strive to hold on to what we have, maintain our present position and conserve the status quo. In dangerous situations, even when opportunities and potentially rewarding outcomes are offered, we are not very likely to rub our hands in glee and say *"Oh good, another learning opportunity"*.

We are more likely to consider how the proposed change will affect us and our current situation. No matter how positive we are towards change, there will still be some perceived degree of threat. If people are insecure, unsure about their future, subject to attack or ridicule, blame or the withdrawal of support, they are unlikely to be operating at the top of Maslow's hierarchy. The way to keep them there (in the domain of gains) is to focus on the impact the reason for learning may have on the lower level needs.

The following examples should be considered:

- Will the individual's earning capacity be affected?

- Will it involve a change of location? If so, how will the individual's travel to work, lunch or other personal arrangements be affected?

- Will the individual's friendships and the other social activities engaged in at work be affected?

- Will the need to learn new skills reduce the individual's level of performance in their own eyes and those of their colleagues by taking them back to the level of novice?

For those of us excited by the prospect of learning, it is sometimes hard to understand why other people do not share the same high level of motivation for it. We see the excitement and thrill that the chance of meeting new people, coming across new ideas, doing different things and having to use our brains offers. It is sometimes difficult to appreciate that other people see the same opportunity as dangerous, threatening, difficult and unwelcome. Yet that is the reality for many people. The concept of Lifelong Learning can be seen as the same as living life on a roller coaster, founded on shifting sands and running in perpetual fog.

SUMMARY

This chapter has outlined some of the many factors that influence people's view of learning. Much of it is governed by previous and possibly forgotten experiences. It is worth spending some time considering what has influenced your and other people's attitudes to learning before embarking on the journey. This is particularly important if you or they have not been involved in learning for some time. Learning is a fragile process and, if approached unprepared and carelessly, could do more harm than good.

The checklist on the following page summarises the points we have considered above and will help you highlight the main factors that have influenced your current view of learning.

The insight you gain into your learning history contributes to your understanding of the learning processes and your preferred learning styles. You are now ready to explore in the next chapter the obstacles that might stand in your way.

How do you make choices?
What restricts your options?
Are these perceived or real limits?

How close and solid are the real limits that wall in your decisions?
What do you need to do to test those limits without taking too many risks or chance causing damage?
Do you have more freedom than you think?

What were your previous experiences of learning?
What factors influence your memories and cause you to think of them as positive or negative experiences?
How can you use this insight to help make future learning experiences more constructive and effective?

Who influenced your learning and learning experiences, directly and indirectly?
What was it about their influence that makes you recall them in a favourable or unfavourable light?
How will this insight contribute to the nature of the relationships you form with influential people in future?

How does your personality affect your approach to learning?
Where do your intellectual strengths lie?
How creative are you, what kinds of problems do you find easiest to resolve and which are more difficult?
Do you think you could improve on your problem-solving skills and release more of your in-built creativity by learning some techniques?

How prepared are you to take risks?
In which type of situation?
What risks will you take and which will you not consider at any price?

What drives you to learn?
What encourages you to preserve your current situation?
What could be done to increase your motivation for learning?

Chapter 3

What Stops Learning?

INTRODUCTION

It is easy to look to oneself and find faults and weaknesses. We are encouraged to see ourselves as flawed and feeble human beings. In our culture, blowing one's own trumpet is regarded as a sin and we are trained to be modest about our talents. As a result any problem we may have with learning is because we are poor learners. Rarely do we consider the role others can play in making the process harder than it need be – unless of course we are looking for scapegoats or someone to blame. Even less frequently do we look to the environment and examine whether it is contributing in any way to the difficulties we as learners may be facing.

It would be wrong to imply that all the causes of learning difficulties lie at the door of others. It must be recognised that some of the problems are due to us being poor learners. Learning skills are increasingly discussed but rarely is any useful definition offered to help us improve those skills. Also, there will be times when we are not motivated or disinclined to learn. There are many reasons why this happens; it need not be just lack of interest or laziness.

In this chapter we will examine some of the main problems and difficulties facing adult learners, including those stemming from the individual. We will look at how disincentives and barriers affect our learning abilities and handicap our development and in doing so begin to consider how they may be overcome.

THE LEARNER

Before we address the external factors that may cause a learner difficulty, we must look to ourselves. As we discussed in the previous chapter, we are able to change our behaviour and alter our view of the world if we choose to do so. This may require a period of reflection and questioning, but change of this nature is not impossible if we want to reappraise and alter our actions and attitudes. However, before engaging in the journey to insight, we need to consider where our personal blockages to learning might stem from.

Experience

As previously mentioned, childhood and previous experiences of learning and learning situations affect how adults view learning processes and early experience informs and influences what we do in later life. Contemporary research tells us that more adults are involved in training and education in the United Kingdom than elsewhere in Europe. But we also know that perhaps as many as one in six adults is regarded as being functionally illiterate. Something must have gone very wrong at some time in their learning history if so many people are ill-equipped to function in the modern, information-replete world. Many people must, therefore, need to improve in these basic areas before they are able to take full advantage of the many opportunities available to them to help them develop their skills in other skills.

There is little point in creating learning opportunities for people, for example, to help them use the Internet if they are unable to spell. The World Wide Web may be able to cope with English and American versions of words but it is very unforgiving of transpositions or misspellings. The development of financial management skills requires a basic level of numeracy and most supervisors are required to check documents such as timesheets or fill in forms of some kind. In addition to these basic skills, learning new ones demands a certain level of self-confidence. For anyone aware of deficiencies in such fundamental areas, learning anything else can appear a massive mountain to be climbed.

Most of us move into employment totally unaware of the skills we have developed as learners. Unconscious of the talents we have developed and possibly without opportunities to use them at work, it is not surprising that they fall into disrepair and eventually get lost altogether. Returning to learning at a later time can be hard work. We will return to the question of the skills required to be an effective learner and how they can be retained or renewed again later. The first step to recognising and developing these skills is seeing yourself as a learner.

Self-image

Having learning needs, to some people, is an admission of weakness and failure. The popular image, certainly until comparatively recently, of a learner is someone sitting at a desk in a classroom or "at the feet" of someone who knows more or can do something better than they. There is a relationship and a dynamic of power, with the learner in a position of weakness and vulnerability. Their lack of ability and skill makes them exposed and deficient in some way. The expert has control over the process and so the learner depends on them for their learning.

Recent attempts to create and foster a learning climate have been aimed at changing this image. Rather than being weak, the admission of learning needs is portrayed as strength. A consumer in a marketplace anxious for their business, the learner is presented as someone with a sophisticated degree of insight and self-awareness. Learners are powerful, not weak, for they know what they need to learn to enable them to deal effectively with the demands being made of them. They have a sense of humility, as they are able to recognise, without shame or embarrassment, the areas where improvements or changes to behaviour are needed so they can work better.

The way in which we see ourselves is influenced by our own self-image of who and what we are. It is also influenced by the culture found in the social group to which we belong. It is important to recognise this influence, for we are enabled and constrained by what is acceptable and possible in the society in which we live and work. An example of this can be found in the effects personal development and confidence-building programmes run at work can have on the rest of a person's life.

Mary, a shy but able worker was promoted to be a Supervisor. Her manager felt that she might have some difficulty with some of her former colleagues and so concluded, with her agreement, that an assertiveness course would be beneficial in helping her make the transition. What the manager did not know was that Mary had some difficulties at home.

Mary attended the ten week evening programme run at her local college and found the space and support she had needed for some years to explore who she was and what she wanted from her work and in the rest of her life. She learnt some techniques that enabled her to confront some difficult issues standing in the way of her expressing her wants.

Her manager was delighted with the progress she was making as each week went by. She grew in stature and her increasing confidence allowed her to step into her new role. Her former peers also realised that they needed to form a new relationship with Mary. Those who had hoped for an easy time because of previous friendships were quickly dissuaded of this view.

Her work colleagues were not aware of what was happening elsewhere in Mary's life. Her lazy partner began to notice that the meek and mild Mary was no longer prepared to tolerate the lack of help in the house. Without anger or aggression, Mary clearly pointed out the consequences of his inaction and what he was expected to do differently in future.

If you watch how other people learn, their experiences and the benefits they accrue, it can have a powerful influence on your learning behaviour. If you have seen the positive effects of learning on someone like Mary, it is likely that you will be more inclined to engage in a similar experience. However, on the other side, what do you think Mary's partner (and possibly his friends and colleagues) thought of the resultant change in her attitudes and behaviour? Would they see it as a process whose outcome is desirable? Likewise, if the people you know have had difficult, painful and unrewarding experiences, you are unlikely to want to go through something similar.

We create images in our minds of the sort of people we want to associate with and be like. The fashion industry shamelessly exploits this trait. But for most of us our aspirations are moderated by a sense of realism and as a result we find our heroes and heroines amongst "people like us". Thus famous people with the "common touch" are more respected and respectable than those who seem remote, no matter how appealing their life style may be. The same principles apply equally strongly to the role models of learners. If the learner is like you, facing similar difficulties and with a similar background but reaping the rewards from their learning you want but cannot access, the chances are you will want some – but will you be prepared to pay the price?

Peer pressure

Peer pressure is another major force in learning. If the group value system portrays learning as unapproved activity, it will be difficult for a group member to take part in any form of development action. This situation is well known amongst management development facilitators who often include in the programme sessions to help participants with their re-entry into work and to plan how to apply their learning without threatening colleagues unduly. For the application of learning may challenge them. If you frighten them with new ideas, appear to be a changed person or expect them to make what may be unacceptable changes, they will probably resist. Thus efforts you make to institute changes to working practice and management style will attract opposition, indifference or be ignored.

Those engaged in organisational change know that a critical mass, usually about 30 per cent, is required to make an impact significant enough to sway the behaviour and dynamics of a group. The concept of *conservative dynamism* is helpful, as it neatly describes how groups and organisations subconsciously strive to preserve the status quo. Preservation tends to convey a sense of passivity. Dynamic conservatism on the other hand suggests action, power and movement all focused on maintaining systems, relationships, status, position and ways of working. To shift a group's attitudes and encourage its members to learn different or other skills, enough of them need to be sufficiently convinced that it is worth a try. Even when the support of the critical mass is won, if the social group leaders (i.e. those with power and influence) are not included, efforts to apply learning may be fruitless.

As we discussed in chapter 2, groups extend beyond the immediate work group. We all operate in several groups simultaneously. These include family groups, social groups and society at large. We occupy positions in those groups and are seen by other group members in a variety of roles. Each of these roles has normal patterns of behaviour and expectations assigned to them. We use stereotypes as shorthand to characterise members. For example a manager, typically, is a middle-aged, usually white, male who is decisive and well organised. Similarly an engineer is also a male who is very good with tools. A nurse tends to be a young, possibly black or white but not often Asian, female. A grandmother does not go to work; she wears glasses and sensible shoes. A grandfather is bald and spends his time in the garden. Someone suffering from schizophrenia is dangerous and everyone who is disabled is wheelchair bound.

Clearly all of these are crass descriptions but they are popular misconceptions. The best that can be said about stereotypes is that they are usually wrong. While most of us know that, it does not stop us using them both in the way we perceive others and in the way we view ourselves. Our attitudes limit the scope of our choices and affect our behaviour and the images and limitations are reinforced through the popular media and in the deep value systems current in society. They hold us back from taking risks, from challenging the status quo and from learning.

Charles was a farm worker. He had done well at school but loved the land. All his family had worked in the countryside; none had stayed in education a day longer than they had to. They all shared the love of open spaces, the outdoors and working with animals. All of the family were healthy and tended to live well into their eighties. Charles, in his mid-twenties, believed that his future would be not too different to that experienced by his father and grandfather. He knew farming was changing and that jobs were being lost but he felt that his natural abilities would help him to adapt so he could continue to work on the land – until the day of the accident.

The tractor Charles was driving was hit in the rear by a truck travelling too fast on a narrow country land. Charles was thrown from the cab and suffered severe injuries to his back. After a lengthy period of convalescence he recovered his health but not his ability to walk. What was Charles to do? His self-image had been shattered. What options were open to him?

Not only was his self-image affected, members of his family and his friends had difficulty in getting to know the new Charles.

This stark example is given to illustrate how changed circumstances can challenge how an individual is seen by themselves and others. This limits what they are and are not able to do, and ultimately can change who they are. Similar perceptions influence our development and inform our choices. We have all made important decisions, for example, concerning our education, work options and career plans, based on our self-image and the image of us held by other people.

Research suggests that occupational groups tend to repeat themselves in families. Breaking away from family patterns can be hard and painful for the individual and family, as can be seen, for example, in the difficulties encountered in the efforts to encourage children from working class backgrounds into higher education. Individuals need to build a new vision of what may be possible and create an image of themselves substantially different from that held by their family and peer groups. To some of the other people in the group, the new image presented by the person may appear to be a rejection of them and their value systems. This can put pressure on the individual who is trying to change. The pressure can be of such magnitude that the individual gives up their aspirations and conforms. Alternatively it may lead to a break down in the relationship, as the individual leaves their past behind.

Self-assessment

When creating a new vision and self-image, we carry out an appraisal of our strengths and weaknesses. The abilities sought in later life may be very different from those rewarded during childhood and adolescence. Take the following two examples as illustrations of how the pressure to conform to classroom requirements can limit future learning:

One little girl, very outgoing and talkative, did not like school –"Too much sitting still and keeping quiet" was her first assessment. As she grew older, she was constantly punished for speaking out, to such an extent that her self-confidence was eroded and she became tongue-tied. As she progressed in her chosen career, she was required to attend an MBA programme. The approach to learning adopted by the local university was highly participative and she was expected to present her work to the group. Assessment was made, in part, on the quality of the presentation. She found speaking at such events very embarrassing and difficult, so much so that she began to avoid them. Inevitably her learning was adversely affected.

John was regarded as a problem at school. He was highly active and resented being told what to do. As he grew older, he was increasingly marginalised from normal class activity, being sent out or made to sit in corners on his own. His academic progress suffered and by the time he entered secondary school he was labelled as having behavioural problems. He was not entered for state examinations and left school as an academic failure. It was only in his 30s and by chance that his supervisor on the building site where he was working as a labourer noticed the genius in the cartoons and sketches that covered his time and work sheets. No one throughout his formal education had recognised his talent for observing and recording the world.

Similar pressures to conform to type operate at work. These again limit choices and affect the ways in which we are seen. Research has found that men and women assess themselves in different ways. Men tend to assume that their success is due to their skill but failure is because of other people or bad luck. On the other hand, women tend to see their successes as products of luck or the efforts of "we" and failures due to lack of ability.

If we are not able to assess our abilities with a certain degree of accuracy the learning needs we identify could well be wrong. In the first example, is there any point in the woman trying to acquire presentation skills until she has done something about her levels of self-confidence? A similar example is found in time management training and stress management. Many people try to learn how to manage their time more effectively without learning how to say "no". People are attending stress-management courses to learn relaxation techniques before they have recognised the causes of their stress and the need for a different sort of action to eliminate it.

Fear

We do not give enough recognition to the part fear plays in preventing learning and change. Inherently, human beings strive to protect themselves, other members of the family, the social group and the species. What we have, we defend. Letting go is risky. Moving into the unknown (i.e. a learning situation) is dangerous. The risks involved include:

- the chance of failure/not making the standard required

- making mistakes/getting things wrong

- looking stupid in front of others

- being judged as less able than others (this often happens when learning style is assessed and marked)

- having to admit inability, lack of skill or an absence of knowledge

- having to stop doing things that you were good at.

To some taking risks is exciting but to other people the danger may be too great. The chances of failing, of looking foolish or simply not being good enough prevent some people from even getting to the starting post, never mind making an attempt. On the other hand, there is also fear of success. Learning involves change in skill, knowledge, possibly role and certainly self-image. We saw in the example of Mary how learning can affect other aspects of your life and possibly relationships. Entering learning can take you into uncharted territory and provide new experiences. The following questions, for example, may puzzle a mature learner beginning a part-time degree course:

- What will gaining a degree mean?

- Will my friends and workmates tease me?

- Will I be expected to know everything?

- Will my current job seem boring and uninteresting?

- Will I be dissatisfied?

- What will I do with my spare time once I have finished the course?

- Will I like myself and what will my family and friends think of me?

Shortages

Even if the appraisal of our strengths and weakness is reasonably accurate and we have overcome our fear, we may find that we do not have the opportunities or resources to learn and develop our skills. Our daily lives may be so constrained and our brain capacity so filled with everyday matters that it is simply not possible to find the space needed for learning and reflection. We discussed above our ability to make choices but there are many reasons, such as the demands of others, economic factors and the lack of information, that mean we are not at liberty to exercise them.

Activity crowds in and absorbs all our free time. It is well known that in the UK, the average working week is longer than anywhere else in Europe. On top of the hours at work, we commute long distances, often driving rather than using public transport. We arrive home, with work to do, family commitments to honour and domestic chores to complete. Weekends are spent recovering, doing essential tasks, shopping and perhaps indulging in some form of recreation. Where in this busy seven-day cycle is there time for learning? Learning needs resources, possibly other people of a like inclination and above all, time to think. For those out of employment, activity still expands to fill the time available. We occupy ourselves with routines and tasks that gradually become essential. Releasing ourselves from these demands determination and effort.

As well as being time-poor, we are increasingly living under undue pressure and becoming stressed. A certain level of stress is stimulating, but excessive amounts have adverse effects. Stress is competing with the common cold and backache as a main cause of absence from work. The stresses of modern living are complex, springing from many other sources besides work. The pace of change, new inventions and technological developments seem to be exponential, growing not like Topsy but like microbes. Mobile phones five years ago were the toys of yuppies. Now they are essential tools for everyone, from children to older people. Using the Internet and communicating across the world are everyday activities for many people. Information is increasingly accessible and Freedom of Information a major political issue. But too much information leads to overload. In other words, the brain is faced with too much to be able to process it all effectively. It becomes very difficult to select and decide what to use and what to reject. Metaphorically, it is the same as being presented with a buffet comprised of dishes from many different types of cuisine, none of which you have experienced before. Where do you start? What do you leave?

Is being overloaded worse or better than not having enough information? One reason given by many for not taking up learning activities is simply that they do not know how to access them. They have no contact with those people who "gate-keep" the way in. They do not know there are sources of information (such as the local library or college). They think the Careers Service is for children and young people and they have never heard of the Learning and Skills Councils. Even if they have, they believe they exist for companies not individuals. The jobcentres are for those out of work; they have no role in providing information about learning. Some of the words used to describe learning activities not based in a classroom have little, if any meaning to those outside the system. Correspondence courses are perhaps familiar, but they are not as common as they used to be. "Open Learning" is a term often used for drop-in centres and although the Open University has done a great deal to create opportunities for people to learn at home, what is involved is not that well known. As for distance learning – does that mean a place far away?

Information and communication technology has enormously increased the opportunities for learning and has provided some superb resources. Sadly many of these are expensive and they have only recently become available in public locations. Moreover, you need to learn how to use them technically before you can begin to look at the content. Much more still needs to be done to inform people about learning methods and resources if they are to make the most of them.

Even if we have all the information we need to choose what and how to learn, we are still, and always will be, limited by our intellectual ability. We discussed in chapter 2 the nature of the intellect. While the human brain is rarely used to its full capacity, that capacity is not infinite. We are all different and part of our appraisal of strengths and weaknesses should include a realistic assessment of what may be beyond our grasp. For example, some people are good at detail. They can concentrate on the minutiae of a job and achieve 99 per cent accuracy by taking a long time. Others are good at broad brushing and can move large quantities of work but their level of accuracy is not high. Expecting one to learn the other's skills is not necessarily reasonable.

Finally, we must remember that we all have the right to choose whether to learn or not. There is a danger, in the current climate of learning for all, of seeing those who decide that they do not want to learn as Luddites, unenlightened or just plain ignorant. This is neither true nor fair, providing the person has made their decision on the basis of a consideration of the benefits and difficulties involved. Too often the decision not to engage in learning is a mask hiding fear or lack of information. However, if the decision has been thought about carefully, it deserves to be respected.

OTHERS

We have mentioned already the influence others have on our choices and how, as role models, they provide examples for "social learning". Other people's image of us and their expectations also determine whether we engage in learning or not. In addition to indirect influence, they can also have a direct effect on our attitude to and involvement in learning.

Bertram knew his job. He had been apprenticed trained by the best and had worked at the factory, man and boy. He knew the ropes and everyone knew he knew everything about how the company ran. He had been promoted to chargehand in the 1980's when the company had been taken over. When it retooled, he was sent on a course to learn how the new machines worked and was regarded as the expert. If anything went wrong, Bert sorted it out. If he was not there, the job had to wait. But this was never a problem. He did not have a day off.

Bert had kept his knowledge to himself. He would show the new mechanics and machinists how to operate the machines but faultfinding, if there was a problem, maintenance and repair were his field. He kept the specialist tools in his locker. This was, he claimed, because the tools were expensive, the machines were complicated and the chances of making a mistake were high. And that would mean, of course, that the machine was out of action longer and matters could be made worse. Bert liked to feel indispensable.

> *This had been the situation for the last twenty years and had not caused any problem. The management knew all about Bert's methods but had not seen any reason to confront Bert's attitude. Of course they were aware of and concerned with the possible vulnerability but it was thought that upsetting Bert would create a bigger problem than the one they were trying to solve. In any case, Bert was so reliable and had never let the company down. Until the day he had a heart attack.*

How many companies are dependent on a few people who possess knowledge critical for effective operation? Recently, there has been increased recognition of the damage caused by premature retirements and how the lack of training has led to the loss of essential know-how. But what is being done in practice to help people like Bert share their knowledge?

The next example shows how a similar result can come from a different cause.

> *Elfred knew her stuff. She had obtained a first class honours degree in business studies and when she was awarded the MBA she won a national prize. She was very pleased when she was appointed operations manager for a bus company. A real achievement. She started work with a determination to modernise the way in which routes were planned and to introduce modern technology. She very successfully won the support of her staff and the respect of her colleagues.*
>
> *She investigated, planned and carefully considered the possible options, put forward the best options and gained the approval of the board. She led the implementation team personally making sure that she knew how every aspect of the new systems worked. As time passed members of the team left the employ of the company and were replaced by new people. Eventually Elfred was the only one left who knew how the system worked in detail.*
>
> *The new staff were keen to learn but Elfred had come to find that her position as The Expert was satisfying. The new employees were very bright and had far better IT skills than*

she. She was worried that they would eclipse her. The more worried she became, the less she told her staff. Her initial open management style was replaced by what her, now less than supportive, staff called "mushroom management". She became very reluctant to let her staff experiment and found reasons why they should not attend training courses. Staff, realising they were not developing, began to move on and within a year all the newly appointed members of the team had left. And questions were being asked about Elfred's management abilities.

Bad management is evidenced in the failure to invest in staff training and development. This failure can be systemic – part of the organisation's way of being. But often it is the result of individual manager's behaviour. Examples of this include:

Discouragement

As with the two examples above, for a range of motives, managers can positively discourage other people's learning and erect barriers to stand in their way. Staff can be forbidden from engaging in learning or they can find that "good" excuses are found for them not doing so. The need for change can be rubbished and the individual can be made to appear disloyal or seen as a troublemaker.

Lack of support and encouragement

Rather than direct, open objections, managers can effectively pour cold water on the learning efforts of their staff. Comments such as "Well you can have a go, if you want. But it won't work. We tried it before" are designed to make all but the most determined give up.

Badly given feedback

Feedback can be given badly and bad feedback can be given. In the first case, the way the manager gives feedback to staff can be wounding and inflict damage to their sense of worth. For example, general, personalised statements drawing attention to your lack of ability can dissuade you from trying to do anything new. Comments such as

"You need to get a grip" are really informative and helpful!

The contents of the feedback can also be damaging. Factually incorrect feedback or the wrong sort of guidance can send you off in the wrong direction. For example telling you that your work is not to standard when really there is nothing wrong with it can wreck self-confidence. More damage can be done by advising you how to "improve" your work in the wrong ways.

Put downs

These can really stand in the way of your learning. They are the deliberate and sustained erosion of your belief in yourself. In some cases they can amount to harassment. Not only do you finish with a poor opinion of yourself but, if so targeted, you can also become incapable of accurately appraising your strengths and weaknesses, and so unable to identify what and how to learn to rectify any shortcomings.

Do as I say, not as I do

We have already seen how powerful role modelling is in social learning. We copy the behaviour we see far more often than doing what someone else tells us to do. A manager who sets a bad example repeatedly can quickly lower the morale of staff who in turn lose their inclination to try new or other ways of working more effectively. People are not interested in finding out why they are fed up with work. They are more interested in finding ways to keep their head down, or in getting out.

Destructive competition

Some management techniques aimed at increasing productivity, such as performance-related pay, commission or excessive concern with targets, can destroy team working. Staff, focusing on their own personal objectives, will be less inclined to help a colleague who is not doing so well or to share their best ideas. Levels of trust between colleagues may be low and there may be few examples of people working together as equal team members. The contrary may be witnessed as staff compete inappropriately and, instead of helping each other, individuals deliberately set out to damage the work of their colleagues. Tricks can be played and obstacles erected unnecessarily. One individual, often a weaker member, may be targeted and, rather than being supported, may be the butt of cruel jokes.

High levels of competition can also result in staff "playing it safe". They stick to tried and tested methods, knowing that they will obtain an acceptable level of achievement. (The Hawthorn Experiment found that group members set themselves levels of production that achieved an acceptable level of bonus pay rather than maximising their earnings.) Staff may be reluctant to experiment or learn new ways of working because there may be a chance of damaging their earning level or risk the achievement of the targets.

These productivity improvement techniques do work very well in areas of work where staff do not need to collaborate, for example in sales work where each salesperson is responsible for their own customers or territory and their performance is not dependant or influential on that of others. However, in areas of work where staff need to work together and where the achievement of work objectives depends on co-operation, other ways of increasing productivity, such as skills development and open communications, may be more appropriate.

Lack of training and development skills

Many managers have learnt their management skills from the examples provided by the people who managed them during their early years at work. The United Kingdom has had a shameful history of not investing in training. There have been many reports since the end of the Second World War that have drawn attention to the shortcomings in management education, training and development. The quantity and quality of training of operational staff varies considerably. Some organisations are highly sophisticated in their approach and some sectors, for example the hotel and catering industry, have long traditions of both off and on the job training. However, many others, especially since the demise of the apprenticeship system, appear to have lost the ethos – assuming they ever had it. This regrettable trend can be seen in the public and the private sectors. As well as resulting in untrained staff and skills shortages, managers do not have the personal experience of working in an organisation with a learning culture and so have not been exposed to the skills and techniques associated with instruction, coaching and developing.

Many of these skills and techniques are very straightforward and their acquisition can help with other aspects of management, for example communications and delegation. They also make managing performance far more straightforward and forward looking. We will be looking at some of these in chapter 5, where they are described in greater depth.[1]

ENVIRONMENT

When we use the word "environment" in the context of work we can mean either the physical or the emotional environment. The physical environment includes the layout, furniture, equipment as well as other factors such as the systems and equipment used, heating, lighting, ventilation and hazards.

The emotional environment is the atmosphere and includes the management style used by the manager as well as the organisation's management ethos, the degree of team working and relationships between colleagues and customers, and the overall nature of the organisation.

Physical environment

Saying that the physical layout of your workspace could stand in the way of your learning may seem petty. But there has been some research into how factors such as light, heating and even colour can influence morale and motivation. We know that if we feel demoralised or unmotivated, one of the last things we are inclined to do is learn. Getting these factors right will not automatically lead to high levels of learning, but getting them wrong is likely to result in the opposite.

Hertzberg identified the factors that lead to and sustain increased levels of motivation.[2] These he called the *motivators*. He also identified those that may result in dissatisfaction. These are the *hygiene* factors, which include the working environment. While they are not conducive

---

[1] See also Dale, M, *Developing Management Skills* (London: Kogan Page) 1999.

[2] Hertzberg, F, "One more time: how do you motivate employees?" *Harvard Business Review* (1968), Jan-Feb.

to the individual's sense of well being, they can result in bad feelings about work that last for quite a long time. More important, though, than working conditions, he found company policy and administration to have deep and lasting affects.

Systems

Salaman also noted how organisational structures and systems can stand in the way of innovation.[3] For example the use of historical indicators as a basis for promotion and the appraisal of success can prevent individuals wishing to progress in the hierarchy from seeking new ideas. This situation is made worse in organisations whose stated ambition is to be at the leading edge in their sector but use historic measures to underpin reward systems. Those trying to engage in development and learn new ideas to keep abreast of changes in their area may find that those who conform do better than they. This will simply lead to resentment and a reduction in commitment to trying out new ideas.

It is not just the existing systems that can stop learning. Those not present can also be inhibitors. For example if the organisation has no procedure for review or no way of comparing its performance with others, it will find the identification of learning needs very difficult. Some organisations have found that having systems to investigate accidents and near misses (i.e. accidents or critical incidents that nearly happened but didn't) acts as a way of learning how to improve performance and reduce the risk of such situations actually happening. But those organisations and managers who metaphorically wipe their brow and thank the heavens for their narrow escape miss out.

The systems and procedures and the ways in which work is organised can also stop experimentation and innovation. The following example demonstrates how contradictions can easily become established.

---

[3] Salaman, G, "Why managers won't learn" in C Mabey & P Iles *Managing Learning* (London: Routledge and OU) 1994.

The college had been highly embarrassed. Three students had been found guilty of downloading pornography from the Internet in the Learning Centre and the story had made the national newspapers. The IT manager was told to make sure that there would be no possibility of anything like that happening again.

He and his staff spent the next month erecting firewalls to restrict access to any potentially risqué web sites by preventing the use of certain words or phrases. The system would identify the machine and password of anyone using any of the prohibited words and a report sent to the appropriate department head so that action could be taken.

The Head of Engineering was inundated with reports in the first week. The lecturers were overwhelmed by students complaining they could not access the Internet and found for themselves that essential sites were no longer accessible. The IT staff had included normal engineering words such as tool, bodywork, probe and screwdriver in the list of banned words.

As time went on more and more words with double meanings were included in the banned list and the Internet was used less and less to support learning, as lecturers and students were frustrated by the frequently encountered blocks.

Resources

A lack of equipment and resources can prevent learning. Obviously if you do not have access to a computer, you cannot learn IT skills. But if the equipment you rely on to do your job – be it a computer or a vacuum cleaner – is old, does not work properly and breaks down at regular intervals, you will become quickly frustrated and not inclined to learn how to improve your skills, even in other aspects of your work.

The lack of resources is often taken to mean no money. Very few organisations have absolutely *no* money. Really this means that what money there is is being spent on other things deemed to be more important. Rather than trying to gain more money, which can be extremely difficult, perhaps you should try to alter the priorities. Sometimes, and possibly more often than is realised, the main resource needed for learning is time. Time to talk, time to read and time to think.

Job design and satisfaction

How your job is constructed can also make a big difference to whether you are inclined to engage in learning or whether you have little, if any interest in what you are doing. Jobs are rarely designed, yet some consideration to how the component tasks are put together can make the difference between a job that contains no challenge and is unrewarding and one that stretches you, is interesting and satisfying.

Ali could not understand why so many of the company's trainees left. As Senior Partner responsible for HRM, she thought she had created a super scheme. Every two years a new accountancy graduate would be appointed and given the chance to gain the experience they needed to complete their portfolio required for full professional membership. At the end of the two years, when the contract came to its end the individual would, if a vacancy had arisen in the previous year, be considered for that post, otherwise they would need to apply elsewhere for a job. Ali thought that with the experience gained in a reputable company they would have no problems in finding permanent employment. She could not understand why, time after time, the trainees left before the end of their first year, never mind the second. After four such appointments, she instituted an investigation.

She contacted each of the previous employees and was horrified when they all told her that they had appreciated the opportunity and had expected to gain a broad spectrum of experience. Instead they had been treated as office juniors. The work they had been given to do was the same as that they had done during the first year of their degree course. They had all left because they were bored and fed up with being exploited by the department heads.

Oldham and Hackman[4] proposed ways of increasing job satisfaction by paying attention to:

Skill variety – using a range of abilities rather than simply repeating the same operation time and time again

+

Task identity – being able to see some connection between the job being done and the individual's skills and interests

+

Task signification – doing work that is seen to have some purpose

⇓

The experienced meaningfulness of work

If the individual has some measure of *autonomy*, in other words has some control over the tasks being done and is able to make decisions that affect their work, they will have some *experienced responsibility for the outcomes.*

+

If the tasks are constructed so that the individual is able to obtain *feedback from the job,* they will have *knowledge of actual results.*

⇓

Job satisfaction

Oldham and Hackman suggest that if work is designed with the above factors borne in mind, the chances of obtaining job satisfaction are increased.

Compare, for example, the difference between the following two jobs:

Job A
The role of advisors, it was decided, would be divided on a functional basis with each being responsible for a specialist area. This would enable the staff to develop their knowledge in that area so they would be equipped to provide an in-depth specialist service to clients.

---

4 Hackman, R & G R Oldham, "Development of the job diagnostic survey" *Journal of Applied Psychology* (1975), 60 (2).

The effect of this was two-fold. Clients found that because their queries tended to be wide-ranging, they had to consult two or more advisors. The advisors found that, although they were very knowledgeable, the advice they were given was without context. They also felt that they were not able to give their clients a complete service.

Eventually they began to be frustrated and the organisation found that the highly trained staff were turning over at a rate faster than they could be replaced.

Job B
The organisation could see that its clients fell into several distinct groups. It decided to allocate each of its advisors to one of these groups. This enabled the advisors to understand their client group's needs, get to know individual clients and develop their knowledge across the range of issues typically raised. Should specialist information be required, the advisor would carry out an investigation.

The clients liked this approach as they were able to develop a relationship with their "own" advisor. The advisors were able to draw on their broad knowledge and give the client a complete answer.

Over time, the organisation's reputation for quality service and good client relationships grew and the advisory function was expanded.

While Oldham and Hackman's ideas are over 25 years old and came from America, they suggest some very simple considerations to take into account when dividing up tasks. Frequently, like tasks are grouped without attention being given to the need for variety. The lack of challenge and stimulation, and doing the same thing time after time leads to boredom. And boredom is skull numbing, and numbskulls are not well known for being committed to learning.

Overwork

Too much work can get in the way of learning. If you are overtired and have little spare time, you are hardly likely to pick up a book to learn about a new topic related to your work. You are more likely to want to spend your free time doing something totally different. And rightly so. The brain needs a change. If you do take a break, you may find that a difficulty that has been puzzling you and has resisted resolution may simply dissolve if left alone. Alternatively, you may see the obvious solution staring you in the face when you come to it afresh. Sleeping on something can, at times, be the right thing to do.

Some, however, argue that an inability to complete one's job in the time available is a sign of inefficiency. This is not totally true. Work tends to expand to fill the time available and then, like the fabled Topsy, grows some more. The average working week in the United Kingdom exceeds any other country in the European Union. Does this mean that as a nation the British are inefficient? More probably, it means that the work ethic compounded by the 1980's drive to maximise income has gone too far.

Three possible responses to the need to change have been identified:

1. pretend it will not happen to you

2. do more (or occasionally less) of the same

3. work smarter.

The first, ostrich reaction, inevitably leads to the individual being overtaken by events. The second leads to exhaustion or the individual being regarded as incompetent or lazy. The third involves learning.

The third approach leads to the individual taking stock, recognising the implications of the forthcoming changes and identifying what learning is required. It demands diagnosis and reflection, which cannot be done if you are over-worked, without time and with no spare brain capacity. Making time available is easier said than done. Yet freeing some up is essential for long-term sanity and survival.

The lack of free time prevents people and organisations keeping abreast of relevant developments. The smarter organisations, those able to remain at the leading edge in their fields, are those that have recognised how important it is to build in time for benchmarking, research and development. This is nothing new, nor is it rocket science. Reg Revans, the father of Action Learning, first wrote in the late 1940's about the need for an individual or organisation to learn at a rate faster than that of change. He recognised that if they did not, not only would they fail to keep up to date but they would also begin to go backwards. Nothing stands still; if it does not evolve, it begins to decay.

We noted above that stress is rapidly overtaking other ailments as the largest cause of absence from work. A lot of that stress is generated by over-working and not taking enough time to rest and re-create. Another source of pressure is the rapid and ever-increasing pace of change. Technology, for example, especially that relating to information and communications, is altering weekly never mind yearly, customers' expectations are influenced by world developments and a new season's fashions come out monthly.

The widespread availability of information provides a wonderful resource. It is virtually impossible not to be able to find out *something* about anything at all if you want to. Lack of knowledge and ignorance are no longer adequate excuses. Internet search engines (i.e. applications that will search massive databases) proclaim their widespread abilities to find the answer to anything you could conceivably wish to ask. However, this resource has created another set of problems. How do you discern between what is accurate and what is false, what is relevant or peripheral and what is up-to-date or old? Information processing skills are increasingly essential in the 21st century. But where are the training courses and learning aids to help you acquire them?

Emotional environment

Each organisation has its own culture. It is not intended to describe this in depth here as it can be a complex concept and is adequately covered in standard texts on organisations, such as Handy.[5] It is sufficient here to say that an organisation's culture comprises of:

- preferred behaviour patterns
- shared value systems
- underpinning assumptions.

---

[5] Handy, C, *Understanding Organisations* (Harmondsworth: Penguin) 3rd edition, 1985.

These influence what people do, what they think and how they judge others. Organisations in the same sector can have very different cultures even when the tasks are the same. Compare banks, for example. This can be very confusing to people moving from one to another. The culture found in some organisations fits the definition of a "Learning Organisation" and others have a very different way of working.

These organisations have a culture of keeping one's head down, not taking risks and resisting change. Staff are rewarded by preserving the status quo, not asking difficult questions and not even thinking. A typical comment made by a manager to an employee is, *"I am not interested in what you think. You are here to do the job."* Yet often the person doing the job knows more about it than anyone else and their opinion is, therefore, worth having.

In such organisations, the jobs are constructed badly. They present no challenge, have little reward and offer no stimulation. The focus is on detail with little attention being given to the context in which the job is being done. There is little long-term planning; all effort is put into dealing with the here and now. Staff are expected to comply with rules and not ask difficult questions. As a result, even when they have cause for concern, they tend to keep quiet. Anyone raising difficult issues is seen as being a troublemaker, whistle-blower or the enemy. They are not listened to and their concerns disregarded.

Perhaps worse than an organisation with a culture of secrecy and silence is the one that is "fat and happy". This type of self-satisfaction can take two forms. With the first, there is a level of naïvety and innocence. The members of the organisation genuinely believe that they are the best and are unable to learn anything from anyone. The innocence is accompanied by an arrogance, breed from a sense of superiority. Anyone who dares suggest that perfection can be found in other organisations tends to be met with pure disbelief and then perhaps a degree of sympathy. The person suggesting that other ways or ideas may be superior clearly does not really understand the issue, or the context or the reality. And in any case the organisation had tried it before and of course it hadn't worked.

With the first type, there is a chance, albeit slim, of tempting the organisation to have a go at something new. Of course it would have to be very rewarding and very new. The second type of self-satisfaction is far more dangerous and is known as groupthink. Janis identified certain distinctive characteristics in cohesive, close-knit groups.[6] These characteristics go beyond self-satisfaction; the group members believe themselves to be invincible. This tendency can be clearly seen in governments approaching massive defeat in the polls. There is an illusion in the group that the talent of its members is superior to that of its competitors. They know best and with hard work and good common sense, they will win through. It is obvious: the opposition is weak, inferior, not as popular and generally stupid.

Group members, even if they are, individually, unsure of the wisdom of the chosen course of action, keep their views to themselves. They feel honour-bound to the group and its leader and think they are alone in their doubts. The pressure to conform, in any case, is intense. Questioning decisions and collective wisdoms is seen as evidence of disloyalty. It is not seen as checking out to make sure that all relevant factors have been taken into account. Alternative courses of action or other ideas tend to be dismissed out of hand; they are not even considered, never mind explored.

The key decisionmakers in such types of organisation are protected by a group of gatekeepers who ensure that only the "right" messages get through. Feedback is carefully controlled to make sure that it confirms the rightness of previous decisions. The lack of good quality monitoring and accurate feedback reinforces the sense of invincibility. Can you see any traces of these symptoms in your organisation? They tend to creep in and can erode a group's ability to learn. For if you are invincible and better than everyone else, there is nothing to be learnt, is there?

Some organisations simply get stuck. They stop moving forward and lose their ability to innovate. They are unable to keep up with the changes in their sector or in technology and fall behind their competitors. In falling behind, they begin to lose market share, their income begins to drop and the resources needed for research, development and learning become strained. The good, innovative people see what is happening and begin to move on to other organisations where they are better able to use their talents and creativity. Those left behind, puzzled, probably stressed and without the stimulation, find their abilities to experiment, explore other

---

[6] Janis, I, *Victims of Groupthink: A Psychological Study of Foreign Policy Decisions and Fiascos* (Boston: Houghton Miffin) 1973.

options and learn are reduced. When the organisation realises what is happening the temptation is to do more or less of the same rather than invest in the only way out of the rut – learning.

If a sense of decay is allowed to set in, it is very difficult to stop the downward spiral. Some organisations and even people are able to live on, drawing from the momentum built up when they were vibrant and questioning. Their early success gained enough reserves to enable them to survive, perhaps comfortably, for a long time. There are many large organisations, well placed and previously powerful, gently sinking into decline. People can be the same. How many professional people worked very hard in their youth to establish themselves. They invested heavily in their learning and practised their skills rigorously, until they were regarded as an expert in their field. Then they stopped. Examples of people such as this can be found in very public positions especially when things go wrong. Judges, doctors and similar professionals are held up to ridicule and are described as being "Stick in the Muds", Dinosaurs and worse. But such examples can be found in all walks of life. Those who thought that their apprenticeship completed in the 1960's would see them right until retirement, that a degree would last a lifetime, and organisations who thought that past successes would guarantee the future, are all examples. Can you think of any examples in your circle? They may not be arrogant but they will certainly be unaware of the importance of learning and perhaps have forgotten how to learn.

SUMMARY

We have discussed the barriers to learning so that you may consider if any of the obstacles described above are standing in your way. Being a successful learner requires a number of talents, the primary one being self-insight. Without the ability to appraise your strengths and weaknesses, on the basis of feedback and evidence, in your own particular context, you cannot hope to identify your real learning needs.

Many of the obstacles can be deeply entrenched. Some, inevitably, are personal and unique to you. They can be described as weaknesses or even as flaws in your character. But rather than cast them in such a negative light, they can be described more positively as distinctive parts of your character that sit alongside and complement your strengths. They are only flaws and weaknesses if you allow them to stand in your way. Once you understand where you have come from and why you approach your work and other people in the way you do, you are able to decide what you want to do about them, if you feel improvements can be made.

We have identified possible causes of the barriers that may be inhibiting your learning at three levels. It is important that you are able to distinguish between the obstacles that are causing you the most difficulty. Often we blame ourselves when really other people or factors are responsible. You may like to reflect on what inhibits your learning and might find the following diagram helpful.

However, before you are able to address the two external causes, you may need to do some work on the internal barriers. This will require a degree of self-honesty and introspection. And you may find it hard work and at times painful. But the process is useful, as it will equip you with some of the skills needed to be a Lifelong Learner.

Figure 3.1: What Stands in the Way of you Being an Active and Skilful Learner?

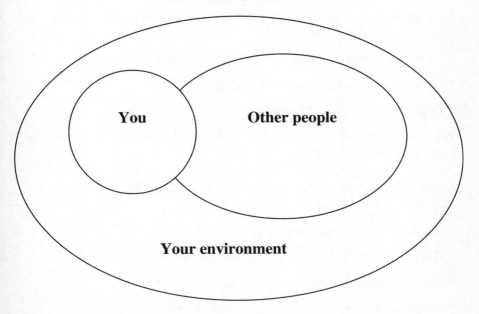

Chapter 4

What Helps Learning?

INTRODUCTION

In the previous chapter we discussed some of the many factors that can stand in the way of you being an active, Lifelong Learner and you were asked to consider what might stand in your way. Gaining insight is an important step on the journey and learning how to be reflective without getting lost in the swamps of introspection is a useful skill to develop. In this chapter we will examine what will help you develop your learning skills further and the kinds of conditions you might need to enable you to use your skills and opportunities to their best effect.

WHAT IS AN EFFECTIVE LEARNER?

In chapter 1 we defined learning as being both a process and an outcome which comprised of:

- a change in the existing level of knowing and ability to do
- an increased insight into self and others
- outcomes that can be applied
- a process by which knowledge will have been created though the transformation of experience.

Being an effective learner means you are able to do all of the above. In practice this means that you can:

- add to your existing knowledge
- develop your skills
- gain increased insight into your self
- enhance your understanding of other people

- apply your skills and knowledge in ways that are appropriate to the situation and the context.

Viall says that learning is "the changes a person makes in himself or herself that increase the know-why and/or know-what and/or know-how the person possesses with respect to a given subject."[1] He goes on to define:

- *know-why* as the ability to place the knowledge and skills into the wider context

- *know-what* as knowledge about a subject or area of work

- *know-how* as the skills needed to apply that knowledge.

Marshall and Reason define knowing as:

- knowing about ideas or concepts

- knowing how to do something, practically

- knowing from experience and emotionally

- knowing from perceptions, dreams, images.[2]

These imply that, to be an effective learner, you need to be able to add to your know-what, know-how and know-why at a number of levels. This notion can be extended by referring to the work of Leary, Boydell and van Boeschoten.[3] They identified seven modes of managerial qualities. These initially were levels of performance but their research led them to conclude that these were more concerned with being and as such they can be seen as developmental steps:

---

[1] Viall, P, *Learning as a Way of Being* (San Francisco: Jossey Bass) 1996.
[2] Marshall, J & P Reason, "Collaboration and self-reflective forms of inquiry in management research" in J Burgoyne & M Reynolds (eds) *Management Learning: Integrating Perspective in Theory and Practice* (London: Sage) 1997.
[3] Leary, M, Boydell T H & M van Boeschoten, *The Qualities of Managing* (Sheffield: The Training Agency) 1986.

Table 4.1: Seven Modes of Managerial Qualities

	Thinking	Feeling	Willing
Adhering and obeying	Memory	Security	Habit
Adapting and controlling	Classification	Control	Effectiveness
Relating	Understanding	Sensitivity	Virtuosity
Experiencing	Grounding	Independence	Activity
Experimenting	Grounding	Striving and Deepening	Rationalism
Connecting	Overview	Widening	Creativity
Integrating and dedicating	Vision	Conviction	Purpose

This hierarchy shows how a learner needs to be able to move from:

• a state of simply knowing and following the rules

• learning how to adjust the rules to suit the particular circumstances

• being able to relate one set of rules of different circumstances

• finding out what happens when the rules are applied differently

• making connections with and between different experiences

• integrating the learning into a conceptual model.

This hierarchy augments Kolb's Learning Cycle and, like it, should be seen as being more complex than a simple progression up a ladder.

The authors picture it as a series of loops. Once one aspect of performance has been sorted, another needs to be developed. Thus learning is ever onwards, ever upward, though sometimes it may not feel like that.

The definition of an effective Lifelong Learner is difficult to construe in simple terms. For as we noted earlier, much of what constitutes learning depends on the individual, their previous experience, preferred style as determined by what that person needs to learn at that particular moment in the situation in which they find themselves, the context in which they are working and the people around them. In other words, the best ways of learning are those that work best for the individual. There is no one simple way of prescribing what an effective learner does.

Nevertheless there are a number of competencies that can be used to guide what a learner may do and how learning skills can be acquired and developed. An essential element in learning concerns knowing. To increase your knowledge it is essential to be open-minded and to actively seek and process information and experiences.

Open-mindedness

Being open-minded means that you are prepared to see an experience as an opportunity for learning, rather than simply a repeat of something you have done before. Other people, even if they know less than you or don't have the same degree of experience, may have a different perspective that might help you see an experience in a different way. A fresh idea coming from an unrelated source may help you look at an issue that has been puzzling you for some time in a different light or make sense of something that happened in the past.

Actively seek information and experiences

This means that you do not simply go through life as a passenger. You must be proactive, inquisitive – talking to people, reading, watching purposefully, listening to what people are talking about, thinking about the issues you hear being discussed and most importantly reflecting. Reflecting does not have to be a solitary activity. You can reflect in a group, using focused but not necessarily structured discussion. Debate, questioning, challenging, playing with ideas, being Devil's Advocate, being controversial are all examples of how you can interact with others to increase understanding. Other techniques, such as brainstorming, nominal group technique, cognitive mapping, use of similarities and hypothesis and reframing, can be used to stimulate creative thinking.

Ability to process the information and experiences

Being an effective learner does not imply that you need the qualities of a sponge. The brain has untold capacities and the extent of its capabilities is not yet fully understood. But it does have limits and, as we discussed above, there are some well-known factors that prevent it working well. One of these is an over-load of information and sensory inputs (experiences). Therefore, to be able to learn effectively, you need to be able to:

• control the supply of information to prevent overloading

• evaluate information and experiences

• decide what to do with what you have obtained.

The latter can include:

• ignoring it

• accepting it as is

• combining it with existing knowledge and previous experiences

• storing it for use in the future.

REASONS FOR LEARNING

We seldom just learn. The human brain is lazy. It does not store information endlessly just for the sake of it. We do not develop new skills out of any context when there is no opportunity to apply them. We need a reason to learn.

Research by Tough[4] shows that people engage in learning projects when:

1. They have a goal to achieve or a task to complete. They recognise the need for knowledge or skills to achieve the goal or task and then take action to acquire the required learning.

    Imagine being told that a week on Monday your employer will be installing a new telephone system that is operated through a touch

---

[4] Tough, A M, *The Adult Learning Projects* (Ontario Institute for Studies in Education Research in Education) Series No 1, 1971.

screen and headset. The new equipment is to be installed on Thursday and your old handset replaced the following Friday. You have a week and a day to adapt.

Sometimes the goal is to alter an unsatisfactory situation. You may find that your present ways of working are time-consuming, bureaucratic and difficult. They may be frustrating and cause you "pain". If learning new work methods offers alternatives that might simplify and ease your job, you are likely to take up the opportunity.

2. They are puzzled by something or are curious. They identify the need to obtain knowledge to solve the puzzle or satiate the curiosity. They will then take action to obtain the knowledge they want.

Some people go to night classes for recreation. And not just courses that have no formal assessment. Some people study languages, philosophy and history for the joy of learning and because they are genuinely interested in the subject. They sit the examinations because they want the certificate, for no other reason.

3. Driven by these motives, people want to learn.

They will then take appropriate action to engage in a form of learning they decide is best suited to them and more likely to be the most effective means of achieving their desired end.

4. They decide what to learn.

Learning without a purpose or some idea of what is to be learnt is like setting off on a journey with no destination in mind and no map in hand. Some people do this and have a really exciting journey; others just get lost and confused.

Reg Revans was working with managers of the newly nationalised coalmines after the Second World War. He was constrained by the managers' lack of time and their perceived inability to leave their workplace even to engage in the learning they deemed to be essential for the necessary increase in output. The difficulties facing each individual differed but broadly they could be seen to fall within the matrix given below. Some were familiar with the work they were required to do but found the setting novel; some were in familiar settings but had never come across the tasks they needed to complete before; others were confronted by totally new work in unfamiliar settings.

Figure 4.1: Familiarity of Task and Setting

TASK

		Familiar	Unfamiliar
	Familiar		
SETTING			
	Unfamiliar		

Even though this was 50 years ago the situation facing those individuals and their consequential learning needs was not that different to the difficulties and challenges facing many people now. Revans developed an approach that enabled the managers to learn from their work and by working with others facing similar situations, "comrades in adversity". This he called "Action Learning".

In devising Action Learning as an approach for the development of managers' skill, he recognised the difference between "programme knowledge", *P*, and "questioning", *Q*. He realised that if you know which question to ask, it is comparatively easy to find the right (or at least a suitable) answer. Thus once you know what skills you need to complete a particular task or you can identify which piece of knowledge you require, the first stage in obtaining the solution is comparatively straightforward. You can then find the course, the teacher, the book, the video, the Web page and so on to help you meet your learning need.

Revans realised that when you are operating in the bottom right quadrant, being able to identify your learning needs or those of your colleagues is not that easy. When you face situations and tasks you have never experienced before how can you know what skills you will need and what you need to know? Framing the question is in itself a challenge to be worked through. Some people are not, for all sorts of reasons, able to frame the question and have to learn how to do this before they are able to engage in any form of learning activity.

Sadly, sometimes certain people are not able to penetrate this barrier and, with neither the motivation to learn nor the clarity of purpose, do not get started on the journey. Others may begin but become confused and less sure of what they are doing and where they are going. They become discouraged and give up. Others overcome the obstacles and carry on. They know what they want and so are able to make sure the means and form of learning are appropriate for them and suitable for their need. They are then able to continue learning and are prepared to learn again.

What encourages learning to continue?

"Nothing breeds success like success". An old adage, no doubt, but, equally without doubt, it is true. People like to see some result in return for their effort. If learning is started for a purpose, it needs to be applied to its purpose. There is nothing worse than learning a new skill and then not being able to put it to work. An example of this can be seen in the millions of pounds and years of effort expended on training people to operate particular computer applications when they have no immediate use for them or no computer on which to practise.

Tough found that the most common reason for learning was the desire to acquire particular knowledge and develop a skill so the individual could apply it to a task.[6] This was followed by puzzlement. The simple desire to learn was the least common reason. The logical conclusion is that the individual, having made the effort and "paid the price" of learning wants to see some return on their investment. If they are not able to benefit from the results of their labours or have a sense of failure, they will not be very likely to repeat the experience. If you have ever had to re-sit an examination, you will know how difficult it is to repeat the preparation and revise the same material again.

The outcomes you will want to achieve will vary considerably depending on the nature and reason for the learning. The most popular and expected outcome is a qualification. Qualifications are currency that is widely understood. They can be rewarded in monetary terms,

---

[6] *Ibid.*

they open the doors to other learning opportunities and they are often used as essential criteria for appointment and promotion decisions. Those with no qualifications face handicap in the labour market and it is proven that those with degrees, over a lifetime, earn considerably more than those without.

The introduction of the National Vocational Qualifications and the increasing emphasis being given to occupational abilities has been, in part, to communicate that academic achievement is only one type of result to be obtained from learning. Other types of "know-what" and "know-how" are equally worthy of certification. The challenge has been to find appropriate ways of assessing and rewarding their possession. Assessing knowledge can be done in ways that are familiar to all: through tests, questioning and examinations. Assessing skills is not so straightforward or easy. Observation against behavioural criteria, the compilation of portfolios of evidence and work achievement are typical examples of the assessment methods that have been developed to deal with this. However, they are time-consuming and some skills, especially cognitive and inter-personal, are difficult to see or assess except over longish periods of time or from the examination of sizeable pieces of work. They are also context-bound, so what may be regarded as innovation in one organisation may be seen as a flight of fancy in another. The assessment of skills acquired through experience and informal learning presents a considerable challenge in the overall aim of helping more people obtain valid qualifications that recognise their achievement and ability.

Some people do not necessarily seek qualifications; they may be content with the increased competence and understanding they obtain from learning. They may also value the opportunity of sharing their learning with others. Take, for example, the individual sent on a visit to another company to see how a particular working method operates in practice. They have a specific purpose – to investigate the practicalities of the method, find out its benefits, discover any problems and report back to colleagues to help them decide whether to adopt and adapt the method in their situation.

Others want to do their job better. They learn because they want to use the new knowledge and skills or operate from a deeper understanding and better-informed perspective. They gain satisfaction from being able to complete the task they could not do before.

Knowing the answer to a puzzle is also satisfying. The process of learning can be enjoyable in its own right, especially if the learning group gelled and had fun together. Some people find that doing a task they could not do before is both motivating and invigorating, and practising new skills and seeing the gradual improvement in their own ability is fulfilling and self-gratifying. But learners also want other people to notice the change in their behaviour, the results of their more effective action and the improvement in their performance. They do not necessarily expect grand rewards and celebrations; simple recognition of the difference may be enough to encourage continued learning.

If you are trying to encourage others to apply and continue their learning, you need to be aware of the three critical realities that will affect their ongoing motivation for learning:

1. They will need time and opportunities to practice. People do not become instant experts. It takes time for new information to become integrated with existing knowledge and for comprehension to result from knowing.

2. Their level of overall effectiveness may fall. Changing behaviour may strip an individual of their level of competence and reduce their self-confidence. Practice and the opportunity to make mistakes gradually rebuilds competence and confidence. But these too take time.

3. Feedback on their performance. They need good quality information if they are to be able to appraise their progress realistically and benefit from the practice. This is where your support in the role of coach can be useful.

CREATING THE CONDITIONS CONDUCIVE TO LEARNING

There has been considerable interest in identifying the nature of a Learning Company or Learning Organisation. It started in the late 1970's and evidence of the quest can be found in the work of Peters and Waterman, Senge, and Pedler and Boydell amongst others. The link between learning and the ability to change and effective, long-lasting organisational success was clearly recognised. Unsurprisingly the search was one for the distinguishing features so they could be copied and replicated. Unfortunately, it was not found to be as simple as that, for what works well for one company may fail dismally for another.

There was no one recipe for success, as many of the organisations who committed themselves to achieving the Investors in People award found that meeting the standards involves more than just following the suggested actions. The later research (for example Pedler and Boydell) found that Learning Organisations have a special type of culture that underpins their processes and systems. This includes a particular approach to people which contains underpinning values about how they are treated. These are described in Dale.[7]

The culture found in these Learning Organisations fosters the conditions that support learning. They encourage people to develop their abilities, whatever they may be; they provide reasons for learning and ensure the resources are available. Individuals and groups are supported through change and any dip in their performance as they progress up the learning curve is understood and tolerated. Their efforts and achievements are recognised and rewarded and they are stimulated to make learning part of their normal way of being.

The work is challenging. This does not mean that the demands of the job are allowed to become overwhelming. It does mean that people are aware of the opportunities and threats facing their organisation. They know what obstacles and difficulties may be facing them; they know what risks are likely to arise and equally they can see what rewards and outcomes may be available. They share clear goals and understand what these mean to them individually and as members of the team.

Much has been said about the degree of turbulence in the world today, the rapid and increasing rate of change and the chaos and complexity we need to deal with. If care is not taken, all of this becomes just too much for us mere mortals. Our inability to make sense of it all and the vastness of the challenge can lead to paralysis. An organisation committed to creating an environment in which people are able to learn to deal with new situations recognises this danger and creates mechanisms to deal with all of this. These mechanisms help to control the vast amount of information generated inside the organisation and hitting it from without. They control the speed of

---

[7] Dale, M, *Developing Management Skills* (London: Kogan Page) 1999.

change and manage the degree of impact the outside world has on the organisation and the people within it.

Supporting learning

Supporting the application of learning is about taking risks. What are these risks in reality? The learner may not have learnt their lesson properly; they may be over-ambitious, trying to do too much too quickly with their new-found skills; they may have over-estimated their ability. On the other hand, they may know very well the limits of their competency and want some support to refine and further develop their skills and knowledge. Without the opportunity to practise their learning in real life, they will never find out what they can and cannot do. Neither will you. Yet, as a manager, your success will be assessed on the achievement of the people who report to you just as much as on your personal achievements. If you are not aware of where their strengths and weaknesses lie, how will you be able to deploy them effectively?

It is essential, if the full benefit of learning is to be achieved for both you and the learner, that you give your support, unconditionally. This does not mean that you should say just "nice things all of the time". Being supportive means being honest but not cruel. It requires you to accept that the learner's performance and levels of self-confidence may dip. You also need to be prepared to give them a chance, give them time to consolidate their learning and understand its implications and practice.

Imagine that you have been asked to set up a help desk operation for your area of work. You may never have done this before but you have previously set up new functions. You have been told that you can have your pick of the existing front line staff to create your team of twenty help desk advisors. You have six weeks from inception to the day the operation is to go live. You know it will take two to three weeks to identify the staff and another week for them to hand over their existing task to other people. That leaves you only two weeks for training and dry runs. When you were given the assignment you were told, in no uncertain terms, that your performance in this project would be used to assess your potential for further advancement in the organisation.

The individuals you select are all highly regarded by their section managers but none have used computers before. You know they are all very keen to succeed. You have high expectations of your new team and are very confident in them. As part of the purchase deal, the software company devised and agreed to run a one-week training programme. This will enable the team members to learn how to use both computers in general and the software package in particular. It will also give your people the opportunity to get to know each other in a "safe" environment before the dry runs to be carried out the following week. These will test the new telephone system and response scripts with "dummy" customers.

By the third day of the training week, you begin to despair. Three of the more mature team members have been driven to tears by their inability to grasp even the most basic computer functions. Six others have turned their frustration on the trainers. The software is too complex; it is not user-friendly and it does not reflect the sorts of question they think their customers are most likely to ask. Another group of six seem to be totally bemused by what they are being asked to do. But as they struggle with their own difficulties, it is apparent that they are running short of patience with the "complainers". In fact, over lunch you witness a heated discussion that makes you wonder whether two individuals will ever be able to work together. Two team members puzzle you, as you are not sure what they are thinking. They are very quiet and appear to be getting on with things. The remaining members of the team are charging ahead. They do not understand the difficulties the others are experiencing and just want to get on.

- *What do you think has happened to your group of competent individuals?*

- *Do you think you will ever get them capable of using the software and working together?*

- *What should you do?*

The above example shows how fear of failure, especially when the stakes are seen to be high, can get in the way of learning and working together on shared difficulties. The worst thing you, the manager, could do, in the above situation, is to berate the individuals and draw attention to their shortcomings. This would be disastrous, as it would damage their trust in you. But it would be equally wrong to make soothing noises and do nothing more. Remember you have only two days left and you will not have time to revisit the training during the last week.

One response would be to call a "time-out" to reassure the staff that the frustration and irritation is not unusual at that particular stage of learning. It should not give rise to panic. If they are to be fair to themselves, they must give themselves time to learn. Using computers for the first time can be difficult for some people but others take to it naturally. You might consider breaking into sub-groups and asking those who are having less difficulty to work with those who are really struggling. The trainers will then be able to devote time and give detailed attention to individual difficulties rather than having to deal with them in general in front of an audience. The complainers may have genuine cause for concern but they need to know that haranguing the trainers in front of the large group is not the way to deal with such issues. Ask them to make notes of what they are not happy with so they can be looked at later and, if needs be, allow remedial action to be taken. For the rest, taking the heat out of the group may provide them with the space so that the trainers, freed from complaints, might be able to give them the explanations they need.

Opportunities to practice

In today's pressure-driven world, the opportunities to practice are often denied. There is frequently only time for one go. This is because change is happening at such a pace that there is little warning of its approach. It is upon us and we have to respond. This often means that we have to learn as we go along. And mistakes happen; they can either be accepted as part of real life, as a chance for learning or as a chance to hold someone to account. We talk about having to move up a steep learning curve quickly but do we build in the need for preparation, rehearsal and practice? Do we recognise that these may speed up learning and enhance the quality of the work?

Just-in-time learning may be economical and an understandable response to rapid change but is it the most effective and is it always the only response? Certainly there are occasions when change hits us unannounced, when we are not ready. The reason why it hits the unprepared is because they are not aware of what is happening around them. On the other hand, it can be argued that many changes can be predicted and their coming spotted. Organisations, described as Learning Companies, take part in activities such as environmental scanning, working in partnership and using information. Even if this information is of peripheral interest, it is used selectively to inform planning. Planning and the intelligent use of information are key to accurate anticipation. The organisations ahead of the field are those able to learn at, or more quickly than, the rate of change. They are skilled in predicting and anticipating for it gives them the chance to prepare. During preparation they use techniques such as scenario modelling, simulations and "what if" analysis. They also give their staff chances to learn and practice the skills they need. They do this by:

• being realistic

• supporting the identification of the know-what and know-how that need to be acquired

• providing the opportunities for learning in real time

• enabling staff to understand the know-why

• aiding the development of critical and fundamental skills such as communications, the use of information technology, critical thinking, team working and learning skills

• accepting that mistakes may happen

• providing feedback to monitor progress up the learning curve and reward success.

The example of the help desk team shows how forethought, planning and preparation can enable a new function to be set up in a way that enables many of the bugs and teething troubles to be removed before real customers are exposed to the service. This helps the people involved develop their skills and confidence in themselves and the systems. It also protects customers from unnecessary exposure to mistakes and helps to keep the quality of the service as high as is reasonably possible. Can you imagine what would have happened if the one-week training had not taken place?

Other ways of providing staff with "safe" time to practice include:

- opening service points to customers later on the quietest mornings
- closing earlier on the quietest afternoon
- holding training sessions during closed time such as evenings or weekends
- having time-out or away-days
- ensuring that staff cover is available to enable small groups of staff to be taken out of front-line service or production
- using staff meetings as short training sessions.

Some managers argue that expensive labour costs inhibit such actions. Do they include the price of inefficient learning and poor performance in their calculations?

Apply learning to real tasks

While safe opportunities for practice are important, learning has to be used for real, and real work provides many opportunities for learning. Even so, the early application of learning should be staged and supported. This will prevent any predictable mistakes being made and can help the learner save face. Action you can take to support early application includes:

- Telling customers that they will be served by someone in training. Some organisations have notices by service points, you can see some staff wearing badges indicating their training status, some managers ask for customers' permission for them to be dealt with by someone undergoing training.

- Having a pre-task briefing session. During this the individual will be asked to imagine what they are likely to encounter during the completion of the task, what problems they may meet and how they are going to respond. This enables you to check they have considered the most likely occurrences, not missed anything obvious and that their responses are appropriate.

- Letting the individual shadow you while you complete the task and then watching them as they do the same. This can be followed by a debriefing and review discussion.

- Asking the individual to complete part of the task and check back with you so you can monitor their progress before they go on to the next stage.

For example, if someone needs to complete an investigation and prepare a report, you could ask them first to gather the required data. You can then discuss the sources they have explored and methods used. This will allow you to check if they have obtained all the necessary information. You can meet again after the individual has completed the analysis to consider its thoroughness and accuracy. This meeting can also be used to discuss the format of the final report. The individual can go on to prepare an initial draft for your review and feedback and then complete the whole task.

Contrast this approach to the one where the individual is sent off alone to do the whole job. There is a chance that they will produce a wonderfully written document, based on incomplete data, inaccurate analysis, presented in the wrong format.

Taking risks

Learning, in itself, is a risky business. Applying it for real also involves taking chances. Some people are naturally risk averse. They do not want to take the chances engaging in risk may force upon them. We discussed this tendency in chapter 2 when we considered risk-aversion and risk-seeking behaviour. However, there are times when the nature of change means that even the most risk averse individual has little, if any, choice. It would be unreasonable for any manager introducing change and requiring individuals to learn new ways of working to fail to take account of the difficulties that individuals such as these face. Acknowledging their difficulty is the first step in finding ways to help them overcome their aversion. There are additional things that can help:

1. be prepared to face up to risk

2. be realistic in the analysis of the nature of the risk

3. identify its components and ways of dealing with its different aspects.

Often the fear of engaging in risk leads to unrealistic assessment of its actuality. We also noted in chapter 2 how flawed we are in predicting likely outcomes. We can improve our predictions by engaging in a rigorous analysis of the risk. Take as an example the case of Stephen.

Stephen was a driver in his 30s and the shop steward. He was well used to opposing management and operated from the basic belief that everything management suggested was designed to have a negative effect on his members. To be fair to Stephen, his belief was based on experience of several poor managers. The company was taken over by new owners who wanted to take a different approach to management and employee relations. Stephen was highly suspicious, especially when an employee development scheme was introduced. He refused to accept that there were no hidden motives behind it.

When the well-equipped Learning Resource Centre was opened he refused to attend the ceremony. He publicly stated that the only reason why staff were being encouraged to learn how to use computers was so the company could move people from job to job without paying them more. He could not believe that the company wanted people to learn how to learn and reward them by helping them develop areas that were of interest to them personally just as much as those related to their jobs.

One of the other stewards was extremely frustrated by Stephen's stubbornness as it was influencing other people and making them reluctant to take up the opportunities. Heated words were exchanged. After the argument, the two went for a drink to heal their differences. During the discussion, it emerged that Stephen was afraid of showing himself up – he had difficulty with reading and writing and did not want anyone to find out. He felt that if

> *he opposed the scheme strongly, others would stand with him*
> *and he would not be shown up.*

Once the nature of the risk is identified and the chances of its occurring realistically assessed, it is possible to work out what to do about it. We often worry about things that are unlikely to happen. In effect we are afraid of slipping on a banana skin when there are no bananas about. We do not ask questions because we are afraid of looking stupid when, in fact, everyone is puzzling about the same issue and is paralysed by the same fear.

When we know what makes up the risk, we can work out how to address it. Sometimes, simply assessing how likely it is, is sufficient. We can compartmentalise risk into:

- very likely – over 90 per cent chance of occurring – in which case we must take steps to avoid it or find ways of managing it

- likely – a 75 per cent chance of occurring – in which case we should have outline plans prepared

- probable – a 50 per cent chance of occurring – in which case we should make contingency plans in case it does occur

- possible – a 25 per cent chance of occurring – in which case we ought to know what we need to do to form suitable responses

- unlikely – less than a 10 per cent chance of occurring – in which case, does it deserve to have any time spent on it?

Working through this assessment can help the risk averse come to terms with their resistance. It also helps the risk seekers be realistic in their development of responses and formation of plans. There is no point in expending vast amounts of effort on preparing for the unlikely eventualities. In the same way, there is no point in *not* being ready for those likely to occur.

We see that Stephen's resistance was based on his experience, his status as a leader in opposing management, his concern about being left behind, his personal lack of basic skills and his fear of being seen as stupid. Overcoming his apparent opposition to the employee development scheme and his suspicion of the new owner's motives needs to be tackled on several fronts. He will require proof of the absence of any hidden agendas. He will need reassurance that his status as an important person will be unaffected by the new approach to employee relations and that his role will continue but possibly in a different form. And his lack of skills needs to be addressed in a sensitive and confidential way.

Providing feedback

Your role as a manager in supporting your staff is critical. Not only do you control the areas of work in which they are active, you can close down opportunities for their development. You are also the person who provides critical information on how the learner is progressing. You and the learner may not like each other. It may be that the learner does not really value your opinion that much. Nevertheless, in terms of feedback, the comments you make, the observations you pass and the basis on which you form your opinions do matter. The provision of good quality information is absolutely essential for the learner. They need to know what is working and where further practice is needed to hone their skills. They need to know which piece of knowledge is of use and which is irrelevant for the moment. Because, in your position as a manager, someone with influence, what you see, experience and perceive are of importance. You may be required to assess performance, determine pay levels, make promotion decisions, provide references for other jobs or for discipline purposes, decide who does which job, who to move, who to make redundant. These are all major decisions that could have wider implications. It is therefore incumbent upon you to make sure that the information you use to form your judgements is sound and not impressionistic. You should also ensure that the way you provide feedback is done to the highest possible standard. This means you should:

- give feedback that is of value to the receiver, not to satisfy the giver

- have regard to timing and place

- relate feedback to specific examples rather than general or abstract comments

- share information rather than give advice, unless asked directly to do so

- explore alternatives rather than try to solve the problems
- construct and transmit the message in ways which can be easily absorbed
- focus on:
  - behaviour rather than the person
  - examples which will be of use rather than making sure all the available information is given
  - evidence rather than inferences
  - description rather than judgement
- check that the message is understood and that the feedback is accurate
- remember the receiver can refuse to accept the feedback
- be clear why the feedback is being given; do not confuse the different types of feedback.

REWARDING LEARNING

Learning needs to be recognised and rewarded, both as it is happening and after the event. Learning takes effort and needs effort to keep going, especially when it gets hard. People deserve to be told that they are making progress even if it is only slow. They also need to be told that their efforts are worthwhile and valued. This can be done by the expression of interest. Just knowing that you are aware of what they are doing may be enough. Words of encouragement, empathy and support are also often appreciated. Similarly, telling other people of the individual's efforts and achievement can demonstrate how much you value their learning in particular and learning in general. Some people can be embarrassed by this attention and gratuitous praise can come over as being patronising and insensitive. But this is no excuse for not giving honest, proper and public recognition for hard work, effort and success.

At the end of the particular piece of learning, the individual may receive a certificate, for example in the form of an NVQ. Some employers have seen that an award such as a proficiency certificate can support learning of a less formal nature. Others have pay systems which are related to levels of competency and/or base promotion decisions on demonstrable ability. Whatever formal system is used in your organisation, you, as a manager and active learner in your own right, are in a position to recognise the effort involved and the sense of achievement that can be gained. Sharing the fruits of your staff's and colleagues' success is one of the joys of being a learning companion.

SUMMARY

We have looked at the actions that can be taken to help learning happen. In doing so we have considered what an effective learner is and does and why it is so important to be open-minded. Being open-minded means being prepared to accept that everyday experiences offer opportunities for learning. But learning takes more than the absorption of experiences, sponge-like and without thought. The experiences and information gathered are processed through thinking and reflection.

If we accept that we are all born naturally curious but that for some, as they grow older, barriers limit their interest and abilities to learn, then if these people are to be motivated to return to learning, something must re-engage their interest. We do not just start again. Generally we learn for a reason: because we have a new task to complete; because we are curious about something; or because we are dissatisfied with our current situation. If you are faced with the task of re-motivating discouraged learners, considering why they have lost interest and what may stimulate them might help you to find the best way of proceeding.

Much of this depends on creating and maintaining the conditions that facilitate learning. These include the provision of support, creating and spotting opportunities for practice, allowing people to take risks and providing constructive feedback. Above all, the effort expended in learning should receive appropriate acknowledgement and success should be rewarded.

The next chapter will outline some of the practical techniques that you can use to help you with your own learning and that can also be used if you are providing support to other people.

Chapter 5

Techniques for Learning

INTRODUCTION

The right sort of climate is essential for learning. While it is possible to learn from bad or painful experiences, it is far more effective to learn in a situation that is conducive to the process. But even when the conditions are right and managers are supportive, learning may not happen. Sometimes support is insufficient: activities, resources and techniques are needed to prompt, facilitate and guide learning.

You will have experienced some of the more common methods. It is highly likely that some of these may have worked well for you; others may have been dismal failures. Many you will not have noticed and perhaps some will be totally new.

Perhaps the most familiar is the lesson, the lecture, the verbal explanation or the demonstration. Typically, someone who knows more than you tells you about the topic and may show you how to carry out a task. Much of your learning will depend on the skills of the provider. It will also depend on your level of interest and motivation. Other learning methods can include reading or watching a television programme or video. It is also likely that you may have been asked to complete a piece of work or prepare a report; you may have been involved in a project or assignment to be completed either alone or with a group of colleagues. Do you recognise these as learning activities? These are examples of the informal opportunities that can be exploited to greater advantage.

There are also many others that can be used quite easily without the need for expensive resources or lots of preparation. There is danger, however, in using techniques for the sake of it. Care should be taken not to do something just because it is there rather than because it is the best way to achieve the desired ends. If a particular technique has worked well for you in the past, use it again. But this does not mean you should not experiment and try to extend your battery of methods. However, if you know that a particular method does not suit your preferred way of learning, there is little point in trying to force it. In chapter 1 we discussed the benefits of developing a broad base of learning styles and becoming a rounded learner. But if you find a particular way of learning is contrary to your preferences, there is little point in damaging your interest in learning. Instead, find another method. Many of the following methods can be used interchangeably, adapted and mixed to suit you, your learning goals, any learning companions and your circumstances.

Remember, what constitutes "best" is a matter of opinion. What matters most is that you achieve your learning goals – not that you use the right method.

LEARNING GOALS

We saw from the work of Tough[1] how important it is to have something to aim for. Yes, we can argue that learning takes place all the time but unless it is targeted it will be unfocused, purposeless and haphazard. It will also be extremely difficult to log and demonstrate progress. This in turn will make recognising its occurrence and rewarding achievement harder. But learning goals should not be limitations. If they are constricting you and preventing you from achieving your desired outcome, you should perhaps reconsider what they contain and how you established them.

Generally speaking, learning goals should:

- emerge from a diagnosis of your learning needs

- be expressed in terms of active words. For example:

  - *I will learn how to [speak French, drive a car, complete a statement of income and expenditure, use PowerPoint]*

  - *I will develop my abilities to [chair committee meetings, speak in public, organise my time, conduct appraisal meetings]*

  - *I will improve my [accuracy, patience when dealing with difficult customers, tendency to complete tasks in a rush]*

- have a timescale attached to them. Of course this can be adjusted

---

[1] Tough, A M, *The Adult Learning Projects* (Ontario Institute for Studies in Education Research in Education) Series No 1, 1971.

but you should try to stay within it, unless the reasons for change are compelling

- contain expressions of standard or some indication so you can judge whether you have been successful. For example:

  - *I will learn how to speak conversational French before I go on holiday next summer*

  is very different from

  - *I will learn how to negotiate contracts with our French partners before my visit next month*

- be contingent. This means that you have some flexibility to change your targets if circumstances change. You should not use this as the excuse for failing to apply yourself to the task of learning but you should not be made to feel under unnecessary pressure if other priorities change

- be agreed with your manager. Some organisations have appraisal schemes that include the agreement of learning objectives or targets. In some, these are imposed; in others they are negotiated during a collaborative diagnosis of need as assessed against past performance, achievement, requirements and personal aspirations.

If you have difficulty in turning your learning goals into words, you may find some of the published competency statements or occupational standards useful. The latter exist now at four or five levels for most of the main occupations. They generally begin at Level 2 – the first stage of skill development – which is often the starting point for many people, especially those returning to learning. Level 3 is aimed at those with experience and or previous qualification in the area of work. Level 4 is for managerial or professional levels of performance and Level 5 is advanced. Occupational standards help people learn as they:

- provide a structure and targets. These are expressed in very tangible terms and include indicators of expected performance, range statements which describe typical areas where the work is carried out and underpinning knowledge, if any is required

- monitor progress. Because the standards are broken down into units and elements, it is easy to take on as much as you feel able. This means that you can go step by step and not over-face yourself. You can also assess how well you are moving forward

- allow the learner to compare their performance against the standard expected of a "competent" performer in a particular area of work. Being national standards, the indictors set out what is generally regarded as good practice and may mean that you will have to raise your own performance. In other words, learn how to work differently, acquire new skills or develop your existing abilities

- encourage the learner to record their achievement and compile a portfolio of evidence. This process serves two purposes:
  1. it aids reflection on experience
  2. it provides a basis for another person (the assessor) to give feedback on standards of performance and achievement. Assessment is essential if the portfolio is being used for qualification purposes

- can result in a certificate. In Britain, if all the required units are completed the occupational standards can lead to the award of a National Vocational Qualification.

Some organisations have developed their own statements of competency. These may include occupational standards but often they are expressed in slightly different forms. They tend to be more expressions of behaviour (i.e. what someone is expected to be able to do) rather than outcome (i.e. what people produce as a result of their behaviour). Competency statements can include cognitive skills (e.g. strategic thinking), interpersonal skills (e.g. leadership) and task-related activities (e.g. planning and organising). Some have levels of competency (e.g. beginner, novice, improver, competent, expert). Others contain expressions of quality (e.g. unskilled, adequate, satisfactory, above average, excellent). Some build in behavioural steps which describe advancing or improving levels of ability.

These competency statements are often used in recruitment and selection and can be found in management development and performance-management schemes. Some organisations have used them to integrate the assessments made during selection to induction and early training, through appraisal and ongoing development to career and succession planning and into the reward management systems. When competency statements are used in such a way, they can make a significant contribution to defining common learning and skills standards and underpin organisational development.

Academic outcomes provide useful learning goals. They tend to be longer term and, to someone returning to learning, can seem very distant. However, many courses, especially those aimed at experienced workers or mature learners, are broken down into short-term goals that can be completed in chunks. For example, many year-long courses have phase tests or projects. Some Universities break the Master in Business Administration into three parts, resulting in the Certificate in Management after year one, the Diploma in Management Studies after year two, with the MBA being awarded after the completion of year three and/or a dissertation.

Involvement in community activities is recognised as an excellent way of having different experiences. Some organisations have seconded staff to schemes such as *Business in the Community* as they offer the chance of making a contribution to society and of extending the abilities of the individuals concerned. Other schemes such as *Common Purpose* have similar aims. Many people find that being involved personally in their community provides satisfaction and experiences different from those encountered in their employment. These include a wide range of things such as being the treasurer of a local sports club, participation in special interest groups or involvement in local schools. Until recently these activities were seen as "hobbies", good works or, perhaps cruelly, self-aggrandisement. The Department for Employment and Education sponsored a research project to explore how these activities could result in valuable informal learning.[2]

Many people frame their learning goals as personal objectives and tell no one about them. The individual may wish to keep this private as:

- they do not want anyone else to be aware of what they perceive to be a weakness

- the goal may be so fuzzy that the individual finds it difficult to express

- the individual may be afraid of failing to achieve the goal so does not want anyone else to know of its existence.

---

[2] Cullen, J et al., *Informal Learning and Widening Participation*. Research Report RR191 (Norwich) 2000.

There may be a host of other reasons why an individual does not want to tell anyone else. While this is understandable, perhaps involving another person can bring greater benefits.

> *Claude had the reputation of being the company's Mr Fix-it. If there was a difficult situation or problem, he was the one sent in to sort it out. He was regarded as being hard, uncompromising and unsympathetic. Many people were afraid of him, others disliked him intensely, most had a grudging respect for his abilities to cut through the trivia and get to the heart of the problem. It was acknowledged that he often found the best way of resolving the situation.*
>
> *The company found his abilities extremely valuable and rewarded him through his pay and status. The only problem was that Claude was unhappy with his reputation. Matters came to a head at the company's staff summer barbecue. While Claude was queuing with his son for a beef burger another member of staff made some extremely rude, personal comments about him. Claude's son heard and was distressed to hear his father described in such terms. Claude was in a quandary – how to change his public persona while remaining effective as the company's troubleshooter.*

You may find that forming learning objectives is made easier if you set them out. Even if you prefer to keep them confidential, write them down and keep them somewhere private. It may be better, however, as we will see below, if you can share them with someone you trust. Like any other type of objective they should be:

S   specific, i.e. behavioural, tangible, clearly expressed and broken into component steps

M   measurable, i.e. include milestones or indicators to tell you that you are going in the right direction and to help you assess how well you are doing

A   achievable, i.e. not be beyond the zone of reasonableness and should fit in with the other demands placed upon you

R   realistic and relevant, i.e. have a meaning in the context of your
       work and other parts of your life and be within your grasp (even
       if you do need the help of other people to reach them)

T   targeted, i.e. focused at an end point. You should know what will
       tell you that you have achieved your goal and what your desired
       outcome is to be.

NEW EXPERIENCES

New experiences can provide the vehicles for achieving your learning
goals. These can include out-of-work activities, such as the
community-based activities mentioned above. They can be part of
your everyday work or close to it. Even listening to the radio and
watching the television can introduce you to new ideas or areas of
skill development you may wish to pursue. Browsing in your local
library, many of which now contain very different media in addition
to the traditional books, journals and music, can also stimulate interest.
More of these later.

Out-of-work activities have the benefit of allowing you to pursue
your personal learning objectives in private. Your goals may have
nothing to do with your work. They may be purely for personal
interest, such as learning how to play a guitar, or some may relate to
family matters, such as being involved in your children's school or
their sport. You may want to develop your skills to help improve
your career or find your way out of an unsatisfactory job.

Some out-of-work activities may have indirect benefits that spin
off into your work or career. For example, being in an "official" role
such as Secretary or Chair of a community group may help you develop
transferable skills. Others have direct application, such as learning
how to use a computer, speak another language or simply building
your self-esteem.

Increasingly organisations are recognising the benefits of employee
development and training policies which may include job-related
training and personal development programmes, learning resource
centres and mentoring schemes. There is little excuse for not taking
advantage of the opportunities if your employer offers such facilities.
Even if the reason for their provision is to help your employer achieve
its business goals, as they are likely to offer you some benefit, there is

no point in denying yourself. Unless, of course, your brain is filled and your energy fully taken by the out-of-hours learning that you are engaged in elsewhere.

Most organisations do not deliberately stand in the way of their employee's learning. Even if, for whatever reason, your employer has decided not to have such a policy, there are many ways in which everyday work can be used to underpin your development and advancement. Every job contains the risk of change. It is no longer a truism to say that nothing stands still – this is reality.

Some people maintain that they do not want to learn or change. They are content to go to work, do their job to the best of their ability and earn enough money to enable them to pursue their out-of-work interests and have good relationships with their colleagues. However, there is a danger of stagnation, monotony and boredom. Some form of stimulation is necessary to maintain attention and interest. Without these there is a danger of performance falling off and failing to reach the standard required for safe working and output. Production line companies introduced job rotation and enrichment schemes to introduce some variety into what were essentially mechanistic jobs. These types of jobs are now found less often as most require a wider range of skills and are subject to change. New machines, methods and systems, products, customers – even new managers and staff – prevent things from standing still for very long.

Mistakes and untoward incidents are very rich sources of learning. Some of these, sadly, we would all prefer not to have happened. Reason conducted research into the causes of some of the world's recent major disasters to see if the root causes could be found.[3] Reason found that, as systems and groupings of people become more complex, the possibility of latent hazards increases. These risks are those in-built into systems as new routines, pieces of equipment or processes are added without any one person being aware of what is being done. As more people contribute, what has been done to the system, why and what effect it might have in other areas becomes obscured. The interactions and links become so sophisticated that no individual is able to understand the whole. When things go wrong, no one person is to blame. The failure is due to systemic not human error. Many accidents are predictable and could be avoided if people trained together, talked to each other and kept proper records. This is why it

---

[3] Reason, J, *Human Error* (Cambridge: Cambridge University Press) 1990.

is so important to record what has happened and why and, more importantly, to learn from slips, mistakes and near misses.

Fortunately, the chance of a real catastrophe happening is slim and the risk should not prevent people and organisations from making experiments. Moving forward involves taking calculated risks and part of calculating the exact nature of the risk involves assessing what learning is needed to reduce that risk.

Sophie, the Managing director of a small catering company, was considering what the Internet could offer her organisation. Her level of computer use was limited to simple word processing. The finance director used a spreadsheet for the accounts and the chef used one for stock control. No one in the company had advanced skills. But Sophie had attended a presentation at the chamber of Commerce and was intrigued by the potential for promotion and mail order.

Her company was doing OK. It had a few contracts for in-house catering and its reputation as high quality supplier meant that it had built up a customer base for special events. The chef had previously worked in confectionery and was a very good all-rounder. Sadly there was little demand locally for his special skills. For a while Sophie and her team had wondered if his abilities might be a way of enabling them to specialise in a niche that would be a beneficial addition to their activities. Would Internet mail order be the way in?

Sophie was worried, however. She had heard about viruses, hackers, pornography, staff spending hours on the net following personal interests, running up huge bills and not doing their work and the massive losses incurred by some DotComs. Was it worth the risk? She was mulling matters over with her teenage children one evening when Simone said "Why don't you go on a course and find out more about it Mum? Then you will know whether the risks outweigh the benefits for real." The next day, Sophie's secretary contacted the TEC, found a suitable course and booked her boss a place. A month later Sophie presented a cost and benefits analysis to her board and the decision, to the delight of the chef, was made to proceed.

We saw earlier that often we are not good at assessing the real size of risk. Even when the risk has been tested and assessed, because it may not be well understood we may not realistically appraise its size and nature. Lack of comprehension and confusion are often treated as being part of the risk rather than being part of the learning. Can you remember learning to drive? The number of things you had to remember to do made the whole task complicated, confusing and dangerous. As you gained in experience, your confidence and understanding of what was happening around you increased and your perception of the dangers of the road decreased.

One way of dealing with new areas of work and assessing the risks involved in change is called *Action Research*. This term means simply what it says it is – you carry out research as part of your everyday actions and work – and comprises the following stages:

1. you are confronted by a problem, a new challenge or task you have not encountered before (the question to be researched)

2. you do not know how to deal with it

3. you define the terms of the question, for example, by describing its nature, what it is not, its boundaries

4. you decide how you are going to explore the question to distinguish, for example, symptoms from causes, its parameters and size

5. you identify criteria by which you will select the solution(s)

6. you decide what information and help you need to answer the question

7. you identify a series of options that may fit your criteria

8. you weigh the options against the criteria by testing the pros and cons of each

9. you choose the "best" option, that is the one that achieves most of what you want for the least cost.

As part of his promotion to production manager in a company that built and refitted photocopiers, Matthew had been given responsibility for the stores. This had previously been run by the service department as the bulk of the items were used in repairing or refurbishing the photocopier machines already sold. However, as the accountant had some concerns about stock control, purchase decisions and recharging, the MD decided that Matthew should take over the department.

Matthew had never had responsibility for such an area of work before and was a little apprehensive about what he was letting himself in for. He decided that the best way to approach the task of introducing better control and monitoring systems was to construct himself a project. With the accountant's help, he defined the terms of the project:

- *to investigate alternative stock control systems (including computer-based systems) suitable for the effective management of a large number of small, low-cost items*

- *to explore the range of companies who supply the stock items to ensure that the best rates and delivery times are achieved*

- *to set up a system so that suppliers could be regularly benchmarked against their competitors.*

He decided to exclude a separate cost control system from his investigation, as the accountant advised that any good stock control system would probably include such a facility. He thought the best way to explore the available systems would be to contact The Institute of Supply and Purchase for a list of main suppliers and to ask the local Business Link if they knew of anyone who had carried out a similar exercise. Eventually he found himself surrounded by piles of catalogues and the telephone numbers of two companies in neighbouring towns. He had several conversations with the stores managers in these and paid them a couple of visits. These helped him decide what to look for and what to avoid. He also received some very useful guidance about the pitfalls involved in computerising stores systems.

> *He drew up a specification including a list of "no-nos". Armed*
> *with this, he felt strong enough to tackle the catalogues. Very*
> *soon the pile was reduced to half a dozen possibles and Matthew*
> *arranged for these to be demonstrated to himself, the accountant*
> *and the store's staff. Two proved to be clearly unsuitable, two*
> *likely and two they were not sure about. Matthew concluded*
> *that he should write a paper for the MD outlining the pros and*
> *cons of each of the four possible systems, the costs involved*
> *and how long it would take to set up the new system. He felt that*
> *formalising his thoughts in this way would help him (and the*
> *other key people involved) decide whether to buy a new system*
> *at all and, if so, which one to chose. The report, he thought,*
> *would also form a record of the actions he had taken and the*
> *thought processes involved.*

As shown in the above example, action research can solve a problem
and provide a vehicle for structuring informal learning. It can also
contain a way of logging the progress and outcome of the investigation
and be proof of the learning journey.

Informal Learning is the sort of learning that is not pre-planned or
structured. It happens in the workplace and is part of doing the job.
The following activities may be primarily concerned with another
purpose but they also present opportunities for learning:

- demonstrations
- instruction
- planned delegation of tasks
- investigations
- staff meetings
- resolving a dispute
- special projects or assignments
- secondments
- being part of a one-off project team
- coaching or mentoring
- acting as/observing role models

- observing more experienced workers
- reading journals, books and other learning resources, trade literature, watching promotional videos
- training experienced staff in instructional, training, coaching and assessing skills
- using checklists to structure training and feedback, monitor performance and compliance with standards, for quality control checks and for health and safety records
- appraising performance, identifying learning needs and planning how to satisfy them
- sharing information about company performance and explaining its business plans and operating context
- visiting other organisations
- attending meetings of trade, professional or other partnership bodies.

Incidental Learning is different from informal learning. Marsick and Watkins, in discussing the difference between them, describe the latter as "unintentional and occurs as a by-product of something else".[4] Informal learning can be intended and built into other activities. Being purposeful, its objectives can be pre-set and the achievement of a desired outcome can be assessed. The process can be reviewed and evaluated. Incidental learning, however, unless it is recognised as learning, may go unnoticed.

The kind of events that contain incidental learning opportunities can include the above. They can also include activities such as trial and error, debate and discussion, and review and reflection. We will discuss reflection at greater length below but the key to exploiting both informal and incidental learning is the ability to look at your experiences in different ways. This is known as *reframing,* that is, looking at an event or experience from a different perspective. Marsick and Watkins go on to say:

1. Proactive learners remain open to alternative frames on a problem,

---

[4] Marsick V J & K Watkins, "Lessons from informal and incidental learning" in J Burgoyne & M Reynolds (eds) *Management Learning: Integrating Perspective in Theory and Practice* (London: Sage) 1997.

seek competing explanations and adopt an attitude of experimentation, trying on new behaviours and working at the process of their own development.

2. Reflection is the primary tool to trigger learning from experience. Disciplined reflection, challenging one's assumptions and comfortable ways of thinking, leads to deeper learning.

3. Insight alone is not enough. Creating a support system which encourages all individuals to grow and accepts individuals who have changed promotes retention of new behaviours.

4. Transformative learning may be catalysed through expert facilitation.

Remember Claude, the unwilling Mr Fix-it? The incident with the other member of staff at the barbecue was the trigger. Claude was forced to review his role and reflect on how it had come about. In his case, discomfort, embarrassment and concern for his son's distress were the immediate emotions and he could have chosen to react in a number of ways. Some lesser individuals may have entered into a heated debate with their colleague and probably caused a more difficult situation and greater distress for the child. Some people would have been deeply hurt and internalised their pain; others would have born a grudge, content to take their revenge in the future. Claude used his emotions as the motivator for learning.

Over the following days, Claude looked back at his history in the company. He wondered how he had first gained the reputation as a troubleshooter. What had he first done to set himself on that road? What now kept him in that role? What were the benefits and what were problems for him? Who depended on him continuing to act as Mr Fix-it, who would be obliged to do things differently if he did not resolve other people's difficult situations? What would happen – would they just remain? He began to stand outside himself and look at his situation in context. He tried as best as he could to look at it from the perspectives of the other key players, as if he was looking in on a play being acted out. He viewed it metaphorically, from the door, the north, east, south and west

> *windows; he looked down from the ceiling and up from the floor.*
> *He took himself out of the "action", changed his role and moved*
> *the other players around the set. This process, though difficult*
> *and mind stretching, gave him new insights. He could see his*
> *situation through other eyes and was able to take into account*
> *other factors he had previously not considered. This insight was*
> *helpful and he began to feel less trapped, but he still was not*
> *clear about what to do next ...*

We will return to Claude again but before we do, we need to consider the critical importance of reflection. Also important is the ability to spot opportunities. If you do not see them, you cannot begin to make use of them. Learning opportunities are like soap bubbles. They glisten when the light catches them and they float in the breeze. You can capture them if you are quick and gentle but if you let them go they float away, lost from view as the light changes. If you grab them too hard you burst them or you blow them away. But if you hold them gently, they are jewels, treasures to be nurtured.

Never discount the value of *new experiences*. They may seem difficult, challenging or even unpleasant but if you reject them out of hand you will never know if there was a pearl hiding inside. Even if the experience does present adversity, part of the learning will include learning how to use such situations to your long-term advantage. If you walk away from the challenge, you will never find out what you rejected. If you say yes, you still retain your option of walking away later. Never say no to the chance of learning.

LEARNING WITH OTHER PEOPLE

Some types of learning, for example deep reflection, can only happen alone. Most types, however, can be enhanced if done with other people. It is not a case of being colleagues in adversity, rather companions in adventure. When they carried out their early research into the Learning Company concept, Pedler, Burgoyne and Boydell widened the term to include a second definition.[5] The authors have long been advocates

---

[5] Pedler, M, Burgoyne, J & T Boydell, *The Learning Company: A Strategy for Sustainable Development* (Maidenhead: McGraw Hill) 1997.

of Action Learning and the value gained from Learning Sets and Groups, and asked, "Who are our companions – the members of the Learning Company? We take a wide view of who these people might be – staff, users and customers, owners and policy makers, suppliers and business partners, even competitors, neighbours, communities and the environment." In fact anyone who is prepared to join in the journey of exploration with you, the venture into the unknown.

The notion of learning in the company of others in companionship has some attractive connotations. Yes, there are elements of partnership but the concept of companionship goes deeper. It implies shared objectives, the readiness to help each other, putting individual priorities in second place and reciprocity. Mutual support does not mean paying each other hollow compliments. Remember the advertisement for the "things your best friend won't tell you"? A learning companion is the person who is prepared and able to provide feedback about important but difficult matters, to tell you things you need to know to help you reduce blind spots.

The role of a learning companion is to provide support and act as a sounding board. But they have their own learning needs and independent concerns. While these may be totally unconnected and have no common elements with yours, you share the learning process as partners. This may involve sharing trials and tribulations, joys and achievements. With your companions, you can drown your sorrows, share the pain and anguish of learning, contrast experiences, swap tips; you can also have fun and celebrate your successes. You can discuss the comparative merits of different approaches and ask each other naive questions to promote deeper reflection.

When Claude was at university, he had shared a flat with other students all studying different courses. At first they had wondered how they would get on, as they seemed to have very little in common. However, as the months passed they found that they had loads to talk about and firm friendships developed. After they graduated they went their separate ways, but Claude remained in touch with Fred. Fred had found a job at the other end of the country but every three or four months they spent a weekend with each other's families.

The next time they met up, Fred observed that Claude seemed troubled and asked him what was the problem. Claude, relieved to have someone outside work to talk to, told all. Fred didn't know the people involved but sensed from the way Claude described the situation that many were content to let him confront problems that were too difficult or too distasteful for them to tackle. Fred asked if this was a possible explanation. Claude, despite his previous reflections, had not considered this possibility. It was as if a spotlight had put his problem into sharp relief. At last, he understood that he had been taken advantage of.

But the difficulty remained – what to do about it? Fred asked another question: "Was the other managers' reluctance to do with their fear of confrontation, laziness, lack of skills or a combination?" But rather than let Claude answer in general, Fred said, "Think about each person separately. They may all see you as a convenience but for different reasons." Claude thought about this and decided that he would have to approach each of his colleagues individually. He realised that there would be no one quick fix.

At the end of the weekend, Fred wished his friend good luck and reminded Claude that he was only a phone call away if any help or support was needed.

You do not have to limit your learning companion to only one person. It is possible to form a group of learning colleagues. They may be formed informally, with groups of like-minded individuals agreeing to help each other learn how to deal with their separate learning needs. Some are set up formally either after or as part of a formal course or programme. Learning groups, often called Action Learning Sets, have a long and worthy history. When properly constituted and run, they are a powerful and effective way of facilitating learning and development. The outcomes can include the development of specific skills as well as general work-related and personal growth.

Action Learning Sets work best when:

- each member has their own learning project, task or problem – a situation they do not currently know how to deal with

- each member agrees to set aside their own needs to work on the problem of each of the other members. How much time and attention is devoted to each is not necessarily an issue. Each person is given what they need

- group members agree to be open and honest with each other. There is little point in not telling your colleagues all the pertinent facts of your problem. How can they help if they have only part of the picture? Group members share all of their thoughts about the situation to offer insights. The only condition to this is that tact is used and other members' feelings are considered

- group members do not tell each other what to do. They ask questions to enable the problem owner to consider it from different perspectives; they share their own experience to help understanding and ways of tackling the problem; they offer options and ideas on how it may be approached.

Sometimes an individual skilled in such work facilitates the group. A facilitator is not a group member, in that they do not have a learning problem. Their skills include being able to recognise any dynamics at work in the group that may inhibit its working and stand in the way of learning. For example one person may be hogging the attention to the detriment of others by insisting on going over the same ground time and again even when everyone has agreed that the issue has been dealt with.

The facilitator can offer insights on how the group is working and the way individuals are contributing to the process. This, in itself can be very useful to aid the development of interpersonal skills. The facilitator may use a number of techniques to help group members address their problems. These include:

- straight questions to help one member to define the nature of their problem, for example:
  - describe the component parts of your problem?
  - what outcome do you want to achieve?
  - where do the boundaries of the problem lie?

– what is not a part of your problem?
– how did the problem develop (separate causes from symptoms)?
– who owns the problem (in addition to you) – who knows, who cares and who can help to resolve it?
– why is your current situation unsatisfactory, which parts would you want to retain, which need to be altered and which changed?

• creative thinking techniques to help resolve the problem, such as:
 – brain storming where group members are asked to offer ideas. Nothing is rejected or judged until everyone has exhausted their stock of thoughts. Only then are the suggestions evaluated
 – nominal group technique where group members are asked to write down ideas on paper. When everyone has finished, the ideas are pooled by the facilitator and considered by the group
 – similarities where group members draw parallels. They describe what the problem feels like no matter how outlandish. This can stimulate the imagination and free up creativity when people have become stuck in the mire created by the complexity of their problem
 – the use of collage or art helps people express sentiments they might find difficult to put into words
 – "what-ifs" where members are asked to consider what will happen if an event occurs or particular action is taken
 – scenario modelling when members are encouraged to think about the future. By projecting themselves forward and then working back to the present, they are able to see how actions taken today might limit desirable options in the longer term. They are also able to consider how other (external) events may impact on and alter their problem.

There are also techniques the facilitator can use to help the group address process issues. Work carried out by Bion of the Tavistock Institute led to the identification of two distinct areas of group activity.[6] *S* activity concerns the social aspects of the group, the relationships, friendships, while *W* activity is the real work of the group. Frequently groups prefer to remain in the domain of *S* activity, which is important but should not be allowed to exclude the *W* activity.

---

[6] Bion, W R, *Experiences in Groups* (London: Tavistock) 1961.

The facilitator can help the group understand the difference between the two and deal with the barriers that inhibit *W* activity. This can be achieved through the use of techniques such as:

- Process observation when the facilitator observes the working of the group and feeds back information to the members. They may not be aware of behaviours that are preventing effective working. These may include, for example, a tendency to interrupt each other so ideas are never fully developed, or domination of the group by an individual who may not be aware of doing so but the effect is to exclude and prevent the input of others.

- Behaviour analysis is similar but the facilitator either carries out a detailed analysis of individual and group interactions or helps the group carry out such an analysis, for example, of communication flows, predominant patterns or styles of behaviour.

- Psychometric or other analytical instruments allow detailed analysis of behaviours, attributes, attitudes, preferences, motivations of group members. The group is analysed, the results fed back, usually to individuals in private, and then used to inform group discussion, deliberations and insight.

- Repertory grid allows the way group members relate to each other to be explored revealing alliances, sub groups, individuals who are isolated or those who share different perspectives.

Disagreement and conflict in groups need not indicate a failure to work productively. They can be signs of energy which can be used for creative rather than destructive purposes, providing they are turned to such ends and their negative aspects kept in control.

Typically, an Action Learning Set meets regularly over a period of weeks, months or even years. It is generally advisable to agree a timescale at the outset and identify the objectives of each participant. The set then continues until all the projects have been completed or until its members are satisfied that it has served its purpose. There can be a danger of trying to make such a group live too long. This happens particularly when people have developed friendships and have enjoyed the process. The euphoria of success can prevent a considered assessment of the value of such a group.

If, however, members see a value in working together in this way, they can always identify further projects. It is also possible to form *learning alliances* or *networks*. These can serve a similar function to learning sets. The main difference is that while the members of an Action Learning Set meet in person, those in an alliance or network may never meet. They may converse one to one and between each other on the telephone or via the Internet. The latter can facilitate email conferences and dialogues across and between individuals and groups with shared interests. The potential of the medium is huge and offers learning networks a variety of opportunities yet to be imagined.

When Fred arrived home after his weekend with his old university friend Claude, he could not get the latter's problem out of his mind. He had been a member of an Action Learning Set as part of his MBA course and had found it useful. He wondered if a similar sort of thing would be helpful to Claude. It was clear that his problem had a number of tricky components and it would take him some time to deal with them all. He talked to one of his colleagues, without breaching Claude's confidence, about the situation. She had also been part of another programme run by the local business school and through her contacts was aware of an innovative approach they were about to launch. Based on the principles of action learning, the business school was setting up virtual sets across the country. Would Claude find the support and help he needed this way?

Coaching, mentoring, tutors and role models

There are other ways in which other people can help you learn. These include acting in the role of a coach or mentor. There is a distinct difference between the two roles. A *coach* is someone who knows the job better than you do. This does not mean that they can do the job better. If you think about football coaches, it is hardly likely that they can play better than the team players but they know the skills and tactics. They are able to observe what the players are doing during practice sessions and games. They can point out bad habits and provide guidance on how to improve in ways that the players are able to accept. The players may not like what they are being told but generally they recognise the value of someone in this role in helping them get better results.

A *mentor* occupies a broader role. They may be able to help with job specific tasks but their main purpose is to exchange ideas, experiences and give support to the other person. The mentor is not directive; their role is more to ask questions, challenge thinking and provide feedback. The purpose is to help the individual being mentored to identify ways of improving their own performance for themselves, develop their skills and make their best possible contribution to their employing organisation. The mentor does not tell them how to "do it good".

A *tutor* is found more often in an educational institution than a place of work. Even so the concept behind the role can be usefully applied to employment as much as education. A tutor has knowledge and skills to share as well as being skilful in stimulating and supporting the learning processes. Typically this is done through assigning the learner a task to complete as a learning exercise. The tutor may provide guidance on how to approach the task and possible sources of material to assist. When the finished work is presented, the tutor encourages the learner to review the results of their work and the processes they followed. The tutor may appraise the quality of the completed task and provide feedback on how the learner approached it.

Often people learn from observing the behaviour of others at work. We discussed in chapter 2, the way in which role models influence and effect development and learning. As a manager or supporter of others' learning, you are in that position. In accepting this role, you need to acknowledge that, at work, you will have to exercise a degree of self-control and ensure that you model "good" practices. You can avoid the "Do as I say, not as I do" trap by remembering Charles Kingsley characters from *The Water Babies* – Mrs Do-as-you-would-be-done-by and Mrs Be-done-by-as-you-did. If you treat others as you would expect to be treated, you are unlikely to demonstrate behaviours you would not want others to copy.

As a *recipient* of help from a coach, mentor, tutor or role model, you will need to be ready to accept feedback. This is sometimes quite difficult, especially when your levels of self-confidence are low and it can be easy to hear criticism and faultfinding in any comment passed on your work or performance. For sure, some people do not give feedback in the most skilful of ways. Comments may be hurtful and some people make them with the sole intent of causing pain. They can find perverted pleasure from destructive sniping. One must question whether the opinion of people who do this is worth having. Anyone really interested in helping you learn will be careful in the way in which they offer feedback and will have developed the necessary skills. Likewise, it is beholden upon you to develop skills so you are able to receive such messages in the spirit in which they are intended.

You will need to:

- develop your listening skills so you hear what is really being said instead of forming an immediate impression

- accept suggestions as possible options rather than instructions

- recognise that words of encouragement and support are not patronising platitudes

- see offers of help as resources not take-over bids

- realise that sympathetic ears are there to be bent, make use of them

- accept praise and recognition of achievement. When someone says that you have done well, they are not necessarily being nice or telling lies. They may genuinely believe that you have made progress, learnt something of substance and have been successful.

LEARNING ALONE

Sometimes, it is not appropriate to learn with other people or there may be no one to hand. This does not mean, though, that help may not be available. We saw from the example of Charles that increasingly help can be obtained from networks and virtual groups. The Internet has potential for offering support for learning in many different ways, some of which are not yet known. In addition to the development of innovative resources for learning, some of the more traditional forms are still valuable. Some of these are outlined below.

The notion of Lifelong Learning is part of the UK Labour Government's policy of re-skilling and up-skilling the workforce but it is neither a party political nor a recent concept. The need to improve the skill and qualification base of the UK population has been recognised for at least the last ten to fifteen years. Many professional bodies have expected their members to engage in continuous professional development and the lack of management skills has been a major concern since the mid-1980's. The main difference now is that all workers are being encouraged to be involved in some form of learning. The motive is not just to enhance the competitive position of UK plc but also to increase the employability of individuals and improve their economic position. Additional resources are being made available for adult learning and new ways of recognising its many forms and outcomes are being sought. The important influence parents' attitudes and behaviours has in relation to their children's learning has also been acknowledged and action is being taken to stimulate "family learning". Many of the new initiatives and programmes are building on those that have been in existence for some time but poorly exploited.

Resources

Perhaps one of the most valuable resources readily and freely available to everyone is the public library service. Built from strong traditions of self-improvement, the library service provides books, journals, information and increasingly other forms of resource. It also provides assistance and advice from the staff on how to access and use the resources. After years of neglect, reduced book funds and cuts in opening hours, the public library system is being drawn into the new Learning Partnerships and renewed resources are enabling them to re-equip and refocus their role. More and more local libraries are transforming their image as suppliers of light romantic fiction to "bored housewives" into that of Learning Recourse Centres, full of books of all types (including the romantic fiction) cassettes and CDs, videos, self-teaching CD-ROMs for use on home computers, internet access, on-line access to data sources and so on. Better and stronger links to colleges and other providers are being formed and library premises being used for a multiplicity of purposes.

Even with the massive change to the way in which messages are conveyed, the written word is still perhaps the most powerful conveyor of ideas and concepts. Pictorial and graphic images and oral messages are useful but the written word endures as a readily accessible way of stimulating the brain. However, the skills of reading, interpreting and understanding written material are the keys needed to access information and knowledge. Without these, learning anything other than interpersonal and kinetic skills is difficult. For those with the skills, *the written word* is very accessible; the medium used to carry it (most often books) is comparatively cheap and very portable. They capture the complete span of human knowledge and catalogue the endeavours of generations.

Professional, trade and specialist journals carry news items on who is doing what or articles describing current and best practices. Even job and other advertisements communicate news about new projects and developments. *Newspapers*, as sources of information and ideas, can stimulate you to develop a new thought or pick up on a concept that can lead to the development of new approaches and skills. They also contain news of opportunities. For example the National Health Service's Commission for Health Improvement advertised widely in the press for lay members, individuals not employed by the service but prepared to contribute to the review of service provision from the patients' viewpoint. This presented an opportunity for people not previously involved in this type of activity to make a contribution and develop their talents in areas they possibly had never imagined before.

The *Internet* makes similar and different sources of information rapidly accessible. However, it is not cheap. Free access and no phone line charges do not remove the set-up costs. If you do not have your own machine, the cost of cybernet cafes can be high and libraries have to impose limits on use. Nevertheless, with a little practice, you will find that you have access to global information. It seems that much of it is available in English as well as the home country's language. But unless you print out the material, you are tied to the VDU to read the pages and this of course limits your movements. Perhaps the most exciting aspect of the Internet is the way in which you can make contact with other people who share your interests across the globe. This can be done by joining mailing bases, chat groups or by making direct contact with individuals.

Learning packs and distance learning materials are often available for use on computers but they can still be found in the form of video and audio tapes, written workbooks, projects or assignments. Correspondence colleges still exist and rely on these media together with assignments and tutor support. The Open University has the largest number of higher education students in the UK and Learning

Direct provides information on programmes which range from basic skills level through topics such as community action, work skills and traditional subjects and can provide access to other sources. Increasingly, the distance learning approach is being used to increase access to educational opportunities for those previously denied the opportunity. One of the greatest difficulties met by the lone student is the sense of isolation. Good providers recognise this and built-in support systems, in the form of tutor access, regular group meetings or, for example, weekend schools. The Internet is enabling the support to be available on-line at the time the student needs the help and networking between students who may never meet in person.

In *computer-based learning programmes* you typically follow the material, answering questions and completing tasks as instructed. The programme assesses your work, provides feedback and can suggest areas where improvements are needed, giving an automatic, immediate appraisal of your progress. Learning via this medium can be fascinating and full of opportunities for coming across the unexpected. As well as the intended learning, you may experience system crashes and you can find yourself trapped in inescapable loops. Never mind – your computer skills will be developed as well as your primary objectives!

TV and radio are everyday purveyors of messages, examples of behaviours, attitudes and ideas. If you watch and listen with an inquiring mindset, the programmes can be informative and stimulating. They can present openings and ideas you can follow up at other times and in other ways. You can observe behaviour patterns, witness the consequences and reflect on whether you want to experiment with them. However, you need to remember the potency of social learning and recognise the power of the medium as being more than a means of entertainment.

Community involvement provides an opportunity for you to occupy a role different to the one you fill in your work. You can meet different people from very different backgrounds, with different motives and doing different types of tasks. The priorities and challenges can be of a different order and the outcomes can provide other forms of satisfaction. The British Government has formally recognised the worth of this type of activity and has supported a number of pilots from the Adult and Community Learning Fund. Other initiatives aimed at encouraging learning in non-traditional settings include the family learning programmes and the Union

Learning Funds, which aims to involve trade unions in the creation and support of opportunities for their members, particularly those concerned with the development of basic literacy and numeracy skills.

The *University for Industry* is neither a university nor exclusively for industry. It is now known as the UfI and has the aim of creating learning opportunities for people in occupational areas mainly at the lower end of the skills spectrum. It is not a provider, but stimulates, innovates and encourages others to provide the means to help people learn. Its main role will be that of a broker, working closely with the Learning and Skills Councils and their partner organisations and as a source of information, particularly for small businesses and individuals.

One of the main difficulties facing people with learning needs is getting hold of the information about how to satisfy them. Training Access Points set up in supermarkets, libraries and other public venues have had limited success. To try to fill the gap, Learning Direct provides a telephone-based and on-line information service. Information, guidance and advice can also be freely found from a number of other sources, including careers advisors, colleges and universities, and jobcentres. If you do not know where to go or who to ask, try your local public library. If the staff cannot provide the answer, they will know who can.

Reflection

A critical component of learning is purposeful thinking. The importance of reflection has been mentioned on many occasions. If new ideas and experiences are to be used for learning, they need to be considered, processed, stored and incorporated with previous learning. If new challenges are being faced and old ways of working will not suffice, you will need to apply some brainpower to the generation of fresh approaches. This will involve deep thinking and hard work. It may also be painful as you confront difficult concepts and aspects of your behaviour or personality you would prefer not to consider. Yet, as we have already discussed, this type of thinking is essential if you are to gain the degree of insight you will need to form the base for action.

Sometimes, the answer will sneak up on you without you having to, metaphorically or actually, wrap a towel round your head. You will have heard the advice "sleep on it". This can be wise, for we tend not to concentrate on any one task for more than a few minutes, as interruptions and distractions are common characteristics of the workplace. The sort of deep thinking involved in learning may take longer periods of time than you are used to spending on any one task. Letting an issue or problem mull around in your mind does not mean to say that it has been forgotten. Your brain will most likely be working on it at a deeper level of consciousness. Ideas, experiences, things said by others, documents read – all apparently long forgotten – will be re-visited and explored. The brain will be at work to generate a solution while your body rests. Intuition, gut instinct and creative thinking are terms used to describe this sort of brain activity.

While reflection is hard work, there are some techniques to help you and to keep your mind focused and applied. The brain is a very undisciplined organ; concentrating on the task in hand can be difficult. If you let it, given the slightest excuse, it will wander off on flights of fancy, following paths and track ways that appear more interesting than the task it is meant to be doing. It gets even more difficult to control when it is tired or under pressure. Using a tool or technique can help to keep it focussed on the main job. Harri-Augstein and Webb describe several exercises based on self-organised learning.[7] These can be used by individuals and groups to promote learning and behaviour change. One method is the learning conversation in which the individual explores their attitudes, the foundations of their belief systems and how these influence their behaviour and responses to other people. This exploration also helps the learner free themselves up and prepares them to consider alternative ideas and approaches.

Reflective practitioner

The reflective practitioner is a term coined by Schon to describe the actions taken by a worker to increase their professional effectiveness.[8] In this sense a "professional" is anyone who relies on an established and accepted body of knowledge to underpin their work. When following this process, the professional considers the basis for their

---

[7] Harri-Augstein, S & I M Webb, *Learning to Change: A Resource for Trainers, Managers and Learners Based on Self-Organised Learning* (Maidenhead: McGraw Hill) 1995.

[8] Schon, D, *The Reflective Practitioner: How Professionals Think in Action* (New York: Basic Books) 1983.

chosen actions and examines whether the theory is:

1. used to underpin practice

2. effective in practice.

On the basis of actual experience, the original theories can be reconsidered. If necessary, they can be revised and behaviour modified. This approach is the evaluation of clinical effectiveness. Clinicians are asked to found their treatment programmes on the basis of positive outcomes and health gains. Proof of effectiveness is sought to underpin practice and in seeking that proof, the professionals review current working methods and learn other ways that achieve greater benefit. It is no longer good enough to say, "We do it this way because that is the way taught during training. This is the best way. There is no other way. It works." Similar approaches are used in other professions. For example teachers, during appraisal and mentoring, are encouraged to reflect on what they have done, how they did it, what was achieved as a result and why. Others, such as social workers, receive supervision from other colleagues to enable them to stand back and review their work.

Discussing matters with another person can draw out the components of an experience, frame and reframe any difficulty or problem, suggest alternative actions and consider outcomes different from those which other courses of action may have achieved.

Schon also suggested that there are two levels of learning. Single learning happens when the learner adjusts their behaviour relative to fixed goals, norms and assumptions. Double loop learning is engaged when the goals, norms and assumptions are also open to change.

RECORDING LEARNING

Recording the learning journey is important, for without some form of log, it can be very difficult to remember and demonstrate what has happened along the way. The results of the learning, if they are improved skills or increased knowledge can be easily evidenced. Other people can see what you do, can tell that you are able to work more effectively or are applying greater understanding to your work. But if the learning has involved the acquisition of deeper personal insight, it can be very difficult to show that to other people, assuming you want to.

Maintaining a personal log of your learning not only creates a record, it can help you retrace your achievements. During life, much of what has been learnt is stored deep in the recesses of our memory banks, seemingly forgotten. Revisiting previous learning experiences by re-reading your record can restore skills and reawaken interests. It can also help you recognise current gaps and stimulate additional development.

Some professional bodies require evidence of continued professional development (CPD) to accredit competence. This trend seems to be growing as concern about poor and out of date practice increases. Sadly, CPD seems to be often taken to mean attending courses and, as we know very well, attendance is no proof of learning. Keeping a diary which contains brief details of what has been learnt from experience can stimulate reflection as well as act as a record of what has been achieved as a result of applying that learning. This seems to be a better check on whether real development has taken place. The record will contain evidence of practice, experiments, trials, mistakes and successes. It will chart improvements, show what does not work and help consolidate learning.

National Vocational Qualifications and increasingly other qualifications involve the completion of a portfolio of evidence. Again, this records the results of learning in the form of tangible examples of work. A portfolio may include copies of reports written, budgets compiled, photographs of a machine before and after repair, a tape of an interview, a video of a meeting, a testimonial from a customer, in fact, anything that shows what the learner is able to do. There is also space to provide evidence of knowledge perhaps in the form of a traditional test or examination, a completed assignment, or a document that enables the individual to express their views on a topic. It can provide, in addition, a vehicle for reflection on the completion of the various tasks and what was learnt during the execution of them.

RECOGNISING ACHIEVEMENT

It is said that "Nothing succeeds like success". The learning log, diary or portfolio is your personal record of your success and reflecting on your learning gives you an opportunity to conduct an honest appraisal of your strengths and weaknesses. It is easy to list the latter but are you able to recognise what you are good at? Many of us find that difficult. But there is no point in dwelling on your inadequacies. If you have any that are substantial and are getting in the way of your effectiveness, get on and do something about them. If you do not recognise your strengths, however, how do you know where to concentrate your efforts for improvement?

Hearing from others is helpful, especially if that person is someone whose opinion you respect. Many organisations have formal appraisal systems to enable this form of assessment to be carried out. However, it is common to find that people on both sides of the management line only pay lip service to it. A wasted opportunity, for done properly it provides a system for:

- agreeing objectives

- jointly identifying where learning is needed to achieve those objectives

- planning the necessary action

- monitoring progress against the plan and agreed objectives

- identifying inhibitors

- deciding what to do about them

- recognising achievement and rewarding success.

Some organisations align their reward strategy alongside individuals' development plans. Extra money is paid for the achievement of qualifications or increased competencies. Gaining a certificate, an award, obtaining a good result, completing the programme can also be rewarding. To receive public acknowledgement of your achievement and effort can be embarrassing but it can also give you a glow deep inside, especially if it is the first time you have ever passed an exam or been successful in any form of learning.

Even if you are not part of a formal programme, there is no reason why your success should go unacknowledged. Tell your friends and family what you are doing, engage their support and share your success. And, if your learning is a private matter, why not praise and reward yourself. After all, isn't your opinion worth having?

EVALUATION AND REVIEW

Evaluation is often the part of learning that is left until last, as an afterthought. It should not be so neglected. What is to be evaluated and how the evaluation will take place should be considered right at the beginning when you are deciding your learning objectives. At the same time as identifying them, you should be asking, "How will I tell if I have achieved...?" Your monitoring, review and evaluation criteria and processes can then be based on those criteria.

Many course review procedures focus on the enjoyability of the process rather than the worth of the outcome. Generally questionnaires explore the physical aspects and have only one or two questions about the achievement of learning. This is sad and misguided, for some important learning outcomes can come from experiences that were not in the least pleasurable. Often the review of learning and its effectiveness comes too soon after the completion of the event and fails to allow the time needed for the practising of new skills and application of knowledge. Sometimes the true value of an experience does not become obvious for a considerable period of time.

The evaluation, as well as addressing the achievement of the desired outcomes, should also allow for the recognition of any incidental learning, that which occurs from the learning process but was not expected or originally intended.

While attending a computer-training course, Mary developed an intense dislike of one of her companions. She found that the intensity of her emotions were getting in the way of developing her IT skills and she began to dread going to the sessions. She had to deal with her feelings, as she really wanted to improve her IT skills. Learning how to cope with people she personally disliked and to subjugate her emotions so they did not get in the way of other things would not have been included in her reasons for starting the course. However, at the end she found she had acquired useful skills of self-control and increased personal awareness.

As part of the review and evaluation of learning, you should include an assessment of the processes used. We have discussed the importance of knowing which learning methods and approaches work best for you and how appreciation of your preferred learning style can help you become a more rounded and well-developed learner. However, do not expect everything to work well for everyone. We need to appreciate and value difference and diversity for their richness enhances, rather than detracts from, learning in its fullest sense. So as well as appreciating the difference between other people, you need to recognise the ways you are different from them and understand why certain learning methods are not effective for you. You will then be in a position to decide what to do about them. You can try to remedy any deficiency in your learning skills or accept them as facts, valuable and unique features that make you the special person that you are.

SUMMARY

We have considered a range of learning techniques that may help you develop the way in which you learn and your abilities as a lifelong learner. There is growing interest in this area with more and more support mechanisms and resources being made available to help people, both in and outside work engage or re-engage in active learning. Research demonstrates that the pay-offs from doing so can be considerable. Learning can improve employability and earning capacity. It also has less tangible forms of pay-back – self-esteem, confidence and a sense of having achieved something that was difficult at the outset but worthwhile.

Learning can be a solitary process; it can also be done in the company of others. These companions may not follow exactly the same route but is possible that you have the same concerns, similar worries, the need to use similar skills and together you can share the same sense of enjoyment and success. Other people can also support your learning in the role of learning helper – as a coach, mentor, tutor or role model. But if they do, you will need to develop the skill of letting them help you.

We have looked at some of the resources readily available to you. The range is rapidly increasing, in particular as the Internet offers untold promises and potential. If you do not have your own computer there are more and more places, for example employer-provided

Learning Resource Centres, colleges and local libraries that will enable you to "surf" at will.

We discussed the importance of recording your learning to aid recognition of your achievement and to fuel reflection, review and evaluation. When thinking about your experiences, you may wish to use the following questions to review your learning:

• What happened?

• Were your objectives achieved?

• How did you approach your work?

• What other outcomes resulted from the experience?

• What and who contributed to their achievement?

• What worked?

• What did not?

• What stood in the way?

• How did people react to you?

• How did you respond to them?

• What could have been done differently?

• What else would have helped?

• How did you apply your learning?

• What helped you get better?

The answers may provide deeper insight, ideas on how you might change your approach and methods, suggestions and opportunities for so doing. They will also enable you to recognise which learning approaches work well for you, which are not so good and which you are best leaving for other people to use.

So good luck on your journey. Please give others a helping hand as you meet and travel together, in companionship, and remember to accept their hand. Together you will achieve more and your best will become even better.